ARDUINO PROGRAMMING

This book Includes

The Ultimate Beginner's And Intermediate's Guide To Learn Arduino In One Day Step-By-Step (#2020 Updated Version | Effective Computer Programming Languages)

Steve Tudor

TABLE OF CONTENTS

INTRODUCTION 9

CHAPTER 1 CHOOSING AND SETTING UP THE ARDUINO 28

CHAPTER 2 INPUTS AND OUTPUTS 34

    VERTICAL INTEGRATION PROJECTS 40

CHAPTER 3 MODULATING THE ON-BOARD LED AND PERSISTENCE OF VISION 60

    WHAT YOU NEED TO KNOW AND WHAT YOU WILL LEARN IN THIS EXPERIMENT 60
    THE BASIC PULSE TRAIN PATTERN 62
    WHAT IS THE FLICKER RATE? 64
    CHANGING THE APPARENT BRIGHTNESS 67
    NEW FEATURES: INTRODUCING VARIABLES AND VARIABLE TYPES 68
    NEW FEATURES: VARIABLE NAMES 77
    ON-TIME, OFF-TIME, PERIOD AND DUTY CYCLE 81
    MY SKETCH TO MODULATE THE LED WITH A PERIOD AND DUTY CYCLE 84
    SUMMARY OF THE COMMANDS INTRODUCED SO FAR 85

CHAPTER 4 CODING FOR THE ARDUINO 92

CHAPTER 5 ULTRASONIC SENSOR 106

CONCLUSION 109

INTRODUCTION 114

CHAPTER 1 KEY TERMS IN UNDERSTANDING ARDUINO 121

CHAPTER 2 WORKING WITH USER-DEFINED FUNCTIONS 125

CHAPTER 3 THE SERIAL 131

CHAPTER 4 CONNECTING SWITCH 135

CHAPTER 5 TEMPERATURE SENSOR 138

    PIR SENSOR 143

CHAPTER 6 USING THE STREAM CLASS... 148

    THE SERIAL 150

CHAPTER 7 CALCULATED DIGITAL REPRESENTATIONS 155

CHAPTER 8 UNDERSTANDING THE ARDUINO FRAMEWORK 159

    CONSTANTS 161

    FUNCTIONS... 162

CHAPTER 9 LEARN THE IMPLEMENTATION OF ALGORITHMS 165

CHAPTER 10 TROUBLESHOOTING... 174

CHAPTER 11 *PROJECTS* 179

CHAPTER 12 SPEND TIME THINKING OUTSIDE THE BOX (AND THE ARDUINO) 189

CHAPTER 13 TROUBLESHOOTING... 193

CONCLUSION 198

ARDUINO PROGRAMMING

THE PRACTICAL **BEGINNER'S** GUIDE TO LEARN ARDUINO PROGRAMMING IN ONE DAY STEP-BY-STEP

(#2020 UPDATED VERSION | EFFECTIVE COMPUTER LANGUAGES)

STEVE TUDOR

Text Copyright ©

All rights reserved. No part of this guide may be reproduced in any form without permission in writing from the publisher except in the case of brief quotations embodied in critical articles or reviews.

Legal & Disclaimer

The information contained in this book and its contents is not designed to replace or take the place of any form of medical or professional advice; and is not meant to replace the need for independent medical, financial, legal or other professional advice or services, as may be required. The content and information in this book has been provided for educational and entertainment purposes only.

The content and information contained in this book has been compiled from sources deemed reliable, and it is accurate to the best of the Author's knowledge, information and belief. However, the Author cannot guarantee its accuracy and validity and cannot be held liable for any errors and/or omissions. Further, changes are periodically made to this book as and when needed. Where appropriate and/or necessary, you must consult a professional (including but not limited to your doctor, attorney, financial advisor or such other professional advisor) before using any of the suggested remedies, techniques, or information in this book.

Upon using the contents and information contained in this book, you agree to hold harmless the Author from and against any damages, costs, and expenses, including any legal fees potentially resulting from the application of any of the information provided by this book. This disclaimer applies to any loss, damages or injury caused by the use and application, whether directly or indirectly, of any advice or information presented, whether for breach of contract, tort, negligence, personal injury, criminal intent, or under any other cause of action.

You agree to accept all risks of using the information presented inside this book.

You agree that by continuing to read this book, where appropriate and/or necessary, you shall consult a professional (including but not limited to your doctor, attorney, or financial advisor or such other advisor as needed) before using any of the suggested remedies, techniques, or information in this book.

Introduction

When it comes to creating some of your own robotics products, there are many things that you can consider. You will need to decide what kind of project you want to work on as well as the type of code that will help you to get the work done. One of the best options that you can use is the Arduino platform.

When we are talking about Arduino, we are talking about a software and microcontroller that is programmable, open sourced, and will use the ATMega chip. It is designed to be more of a prototyping platform, there is a huge fan base for this software when it comes to building an electronic project. When it comes to working with an electronic project, you will find that the Arduino platform is good for using either as a temporary addition while you work on the project or you can even embed it as a permanent part of the robotic project when it is done.

The Arduino board is also programmable with the Arduino software, which is pretty easy to use, even for those who are just getting started and have no idea how to work with this kind of software. If you have happened to use the C++ or Java programming languages, you will see that the Arduino coding language is going to be fairly similar. The idea behind using this software is meant to be really simple, but there is a lot of power there to, making it perfect for those who have some experience and for those who are just getting started out.

Arduino is also an open sourced platform, which means that anyone is able to use it, for free, as well as make adjustments to the code to fit their needs. This is a really cool addition for those who are just starting to use the Arduino system because they will be able to access thousands of codes from other programmers, or even make some changes to their own codes, in order to make the program work perfectly.

In addition to finding that many of the codes that you would like to use are already available and developed, beginners are going to enjoy that the Arduino community is pretty large. You will be able to go online and look through forums and communities to ask your personal questions related to your own project, to find out new information, and even watch tutorials to make working with Arduino easier than ever.

The Arduino platform may be pretty powerful to use, but it is also pretty basic. You will find that this platform only comes with two main components for you to use including:

- The hardware: this is going to include the microcontroller, which is also known as the circuit board. You are able to physically program this part. You will find that there are a number of Arduino boards for you to choose from and the choice will vary depending on the type of project that you are putting together.

The software: this would be the environment that you use with the board, or the IDE, that is going to run right on your own computer. You will use the IDE to help you to upload and write the programming codes that you would like to be relayed over to the board. Once you write your programs on the board and transfer them over, the Arduino board should act in the manner that you requested.

These parts are able to come together to help you to get the project to work well. You need to make sure that you have some hardware in place, such as one of the Arduino board types, and then it needs to respond to what you are able to send through with the software. We will spend some time talking about the various things that you are able to do with the software in order to get your project to work later on, but both of these will need to be set up to ensure that the messages from the IDE are getting over to the board and working properly.

With Arduino, you need to have the IDE in place before writing out any code. The IDE for this program is free since it is open sourced, which makes it easier to get ahold of a copy. When writing codes, you will use the Arduino programming language, which will be easy to learn and works well with all of the operating systems on your computer.

One thing to note with the IDE and the coding language with Arduino, if you are working on a Windows 7 operating system or earlier, you will have a few steps that you will need to take, in addition to the regular steps, to make sure that the Arduino board will work with the operating system. It does work with the older versions of Windows, you just need to take some extra time to introduce the board to this system to get it to work.

Whether you are just getting started out with programming or want to use some of your skills to make a great electronic or robotic project, the Arduino platform will be able to help you get this done. It has all the power that you need with a simplistic background that helps even the beginner understand and accomplish what they want.

What can I do when using Arduino?

One of the first questions that you may have when you see the Arduino programming language is what you are able to do with it all? There are many programming languages out there and you are able to choose them to accomplish different things, but Arduino is going to work a bit differently compared to some of the others.

There are many great projects that you are able to do with the Arduino platform. Basically, the coding that goes with Arduino is going to travel from the IDE on your computer over to the hardware that you purchase to go with your project. You can use just the board or attach it to some electronic project to make it do some amazing things.

There are a lot of things that you can do with your robotics with the help of Arduino and if you are just getting started with your own electronic learning process or you want to try something new, this is the best platform to do so with. You are able to work with the board making sounds, blinking lights, sending out signals to control what is on the screen ahead of it, and so many other things. We will spend some time looking at the different projects that you are able to do with Arduino so you get a better idea of what you are able to do with this great language.

What isn't Arduino able to do?

As we mentioned above, there are quite a few things that you are able to do with the Arduino platform, but there are also some things that you won't be able to do. First, the Arduino language doesn't have a ton of processing power, so if you want to do a task that is considered intensive, you won't be able to do it with the Arduino platform. This means that the Arduino language won't be able to do things like output video or audio, or even record or process them, though you are able to use it to put graphics on a TFT or LCD screen. If you would like to do some of these processes, you would need to choose a different programming language.

In addition, you will find that the Arduino boards should work similar to a computer board, but this isn't true. It is not possible to hook up a webcam, keyboard, or other option to the board and try to use it because these boards don't have an operating system that comes with it. The confusion with this often comes from a similar product, the Raspberry Pi, which looks the same but actually has its own operating system and can work similar to a computer. The Arduino boards do not work this way.

When you write out the codes with this option, you are going to be using the operating system that comes with your computer. Once the code is written, it is not going to tell the computer what to do. Rather, your computer is going to send this code over to the Arduino board and the board will react in the manner that you wish. For example, you wouldn't be able to use this code to hack into another computer or to create your own website, but it can be sent over to the Arduino board to help it to become a remote control for a game.

Who should use Arduino?

One thing that you will like about the Arduino system is that anyone is able to use it for their own personal needs. Many experts in programming and robotics like to use Arduino because of all the variety that comes with it and they can create their own projects, make any changes to the code that they want, and it has enough power to get things done in no time. Beginners like this because it is easy to learn and you will be able to try out a few of the codes right away to create your own project.

Pretty much anyone who would like to create some of their own robotics and electronic projects will find that the Arduino system is one of the best for them to use. It has a lot of power that makes man projects possible but it is still easy enough that a beginner will not get too frustrated when trying to get it to work for the first time.

Why should I choose Arduino?

So far we have spent some time talking about what the Arduino platform is all about and why you would consider using it for your needs, such as what it is able to do. But there are some other choices out there that you can make when it comes to picking out a board that will control your electronic, so why should you choose to go with the Arduino platform? Here are some of the benefits that come with using Arduino and why you should choose this platform over one of the other options:

- Works across many platforms: the IDE that works with Arduino has the ability to work with pretty much any operating system that you want. It will work with Mac OS, Windows, and Linux. You do need to take precautions when using Windows 7 or earlier, but we will discuss later how to make this work even if you do have an older version.

- Simple environment: when you are a beginner, you don't want to pick an environment that is hard to get through. The Arduino environment is similar to the C++ environment, but has been made even simpler to use.

- Open source: the board plans that come with Arduino are published to be open sourced. This means that programmers are able to come and use the platform and the software, as well as make changes to them whenever needed. This can be nice for programmers who are looking to use the platform but want to make some changes to get it to work for their needs and it is nice for the beginners because there are already many codes available for you to choose from.

- Free to use: since this is an open sourced software, the code is free to use. You will be able to use the software as well as the IDE for free, but keep in mind that you will need to purchase the boards that you want to use for your project. The boards are pretty inexpensive and there are a variety of options so you can experiment a bit and find the one that is right for you.

A large community: the community for Arduino is pretty large, which makes it a great option for you to choose as a beginner. You will be able to find many forums and other locations where you can ask questions, look at tutorials, and find that answers that you need when working on your project.

There is so much that you are going to fall in love with when you are using this platform for some of your own projects. If you are just getting into the world of coding and you want to create a great project, or just mess around and learn something new, the Arduino platform is one of the best that you can choose. Let's take a look at some of the steps that you need to take to hook up one of the Arduino boards to your computer as well as some of the projects that you are able to do to get some great results with this platform.

Terminology to help out

When you are learning about a new coding language, there are always some new terminology that you will need to learn. Before we start to work on some of the projects that are later on in this book, we will need to discuss some of the terms that are popular in many of the directions so you know what is going on. Some of the terms that you should know include:

- Breadboard: this is a tool that is reusable for building circuits. It makes it easier to connect the circuits without having to get them permanently attached to the board. It is also a stable surface that will connect all your components together.

- Compiler: the compiler is a piece of software that will take your written program and translate it into something that the Arduino microcontroller is able to understand.
- Device driver: this is a piece of software that makes it so that the computer is able to communicate with the devices that are attached to it, such as the Arduino board. If the device driver doesn't work well, the computer and the Arduino board won't work together.
- EEPROM: this will stand for Electrically Erasable Programmable Read-Only Memory. This is a computer chip that will be written and re-written with the code that you want. You should notice that it is electrically erasable which is when an electric current will erase the information so that you are able to use it. Keep in mind that all of the information on this will be erased when you use this option.
- External interrupt: the external interrupt means that something that is outside of the processor or the computer system and it needs your attention.
- Flash memory: this is one of your memory choices. It is going to retain the data whether there is power to the system or not. A good example would be the flash drive, which is going to store files, even if it isn't plugged into your computer.
- Digital input/output: digital pins are known to have either a high or a low value. You are able to pick from a wide variety of digital pins based on the type of board that you get.

- Analog input/output: this is opposite of working with digital. The analog is going to receive a continuous electrical signal, while the digital option will focus just on whether the value is either zero or one. Both can be available on your board depending on what you are doing with it.
- Processor: this is the part of the system that is going to take the instructions from the computer, figure out what you would like to have done with these instructions, and then runs them.
- Serial communication: when this kind of communication is occurring, it means that the two systems are sending digital pulses between them at a rate that you determine.
- Sketch: this is what the Arduino code is known as. It is going to consist of the instructions that you will send to tell Arduino how to run. You will need to compile the sketch and then upload it to your board.

SPI: this stands for serial peripheral interface. It is in charge of keeping the data communication protocol over small distances.

Getting started on one of your first projects in Arduino can be an exciting experience. This is a great program to learn how to use whether you are brand new to the world of coding or you are ready to take things to a new level. This guidebook will show you how to download some of your own projects and create them for the first time as well as some of the basics that you need to get the boards to work.

Setting Up Your Arduino Platform

The Arduino platform is really popular and is always seeing a lot of changes, which means that as a beginner, there are always new things that you can learn about this platform in order to make it your own. We are going to focus on the basics that come with using the Arduino platform, but there are so many new projects that you can learn how to use with this option that it is a good idea to try new things out, keep up with some of the forums and communities, and see what is available for you to expand your knowledge with.

At this time, we will stick with the basics of how to use the platform as well as some of the projects that you are able to use. To get started, there are a few essentials that you will need to get ahold of in order to make the program work. These essentials include the Arduino board and the software that will talk to the board.

What is the Arduino Board?

The Arduino board is necessary if you would like to get started on your first project. There are a variety of options that you are able to choose from though and each one works with a different kind of project. This is why it is a good idea to understand some of the basics of the boards before you go out and purchase one, or you may end up with one that isn't what you want. Each board is able to do slightly different things and they may even look a bit different, but they should all have some of the same components in common including:

- Barrel Jack and USB: all of the boards that you can purchase will need to have some means in order to connect them to your power source, such as to the wall or to your computer. Many of them will also have a USB connect so that you are able to hook them to the computer and download the codes to it. You can also use the barrel jack which helps the board plug right into the wall.
- Pins: the pins are basically the points where you will create your circuits when you connect them with wires. There are several types of pins that you are able to use with the Arduino boards and each of them have a different function. There are several types of pins that you can find on your board including:
    - GND: THIS IS THE SHORT FOR GOURD. THESE ARE GOING TO BE THE PINS THAT ARE USED IN ORDER TO GROUND OUT THE CIRCUIT YOU ARE CREATING.
    - 5V AND 3.3V: THESE ARE THE PINS THAT WILL GIVE THE RIGHT KIND OF VOLTAGE THAT YOUR PROJECT NEEDS, EITHER THE 5 VOLTS OR THE 3.3 VOLTS.
    - ANALOG: THESE ARE BASICALLY THE PINS THAT ARE SEEN RIGHT UNDER THE ANALOG IN LABEL ON THE BOARD. THESE CAN BE USED FOR READING ANY SIGNALS THAT COME IN FROM THE ANALOG SENSORS AND

THEN THEY ARE TURNED INTO A DIGITAL VALUE FOR YOU TO READ.
- o AREF: THIS IS A SHORT FORM OF THE ANALOG REFERENCE. THIS IS GOING TO BE THE PIN THAT YOU WILL USE WHEN YOU WANT TO SET A MAXIMUM OR AN UPPER LIMIT FOR THE EXTERNAL VOLTAGE THAT GOES TO THE ANALOG PINS. YOU WILL USUALLY WANT TO PICK A MAXIMUM OF 0 TO 5 VOLTS, BUT MOST OF THE TIME YOU WON'T USE THESE AT ALL.
- o PWM: THESE ARE FOUND IN MANY ARDUINO BOARDS AND THIS LABEL IS FOUND RIGHT NEXT TO THE DIGITAL PINS. THESE PINS ARE USED FOR EITHER NORMAL DIGITAL PINS OR FOR A SIGNAL THAT IS CALLED PULSE-WIDTH MODULATION.
- o DIGITAL: THESE ARE THE PINS THAT ARE FUND RIGHT ACROSS FROM YOUR ANALOG PINS AND WILL BE FOUND RIGHT UNDER THE DIGITAL LABEL. THESE PINS ARE USED TO SHOW THE INPUT AND THE OUTPUT THAT IS PROVIDED BY THE DIGITAL SIGNAL.
- Reset button: this is the button that is going to allow the pin to rest right on the ground and then will restart the code that you already loaded onto your board. It is the one that you will use when you want to test out your code a few times.

Keep in mind that it is not going to reset everything on the board and it won't be able to fix issues if they are there.
- Power LED indicator: this is going to be a small LED light that should be right next to the label for ON right by it. This should light up whenever you plug this board into a new power source.

Voltage regulator: this is the part of the board that will be able to control how much voltage you would like to get onto your board at a time. If there is voltage that is above this set limit, it will be able to turn it away. It will not be able to handle anything that is above 20 volts so make sure that your power source is lower than this or you can have issues with destroying the board.

Each of these pins can be important based on the project that you are using your board for. You will need to pick out the board that has the right pins for the project that you need. Many of the beginner projects are going to have information on which board you are able to use and as you get more familiar with how things work, you will be able to figure out which boards are needed for your more advanced projects.

Hooking up the Arduino software

By this point, you will have the right hardware, or the right board, in order to get started with your first project. It is now time to install the software, also known as the IDE, to make sure that Arduino is going to work. The IDE is basically the environment that you need to have in order to write your code before sending it over to the board and to attach all of the circuit components. Without having the right IDE in place, you would never get the code over to the microcontroller and the board would just remain lifeless.

To download the IDE that you would like to use, go to the website www.arduino.cc in order to find the link for downloaded. Give the IDE some time to download on your computer, and when it is done, you should see a zip folder. Open up this file and then save it to the right location on your computer; pick the one that you like the best to ensure that you are able to find it later if needed.

When this is done, you can open up the Arduino.EXE file and then run it to get the installation started. There will be a few command prompts that will come up during the process so read through them and click in order to get it all set up. Once the IDE is installed and the components are all in place, it is time to start working on some of the projects in this guidebook in order to see what all Arduino is able to do.

Getting Started with Arduino

Since this is a platform that is widely popular and is constantly expanding and changing, it is important to keep in mind that you will have to continue learning about the programming language as changes to it occur. To begin with though, we are going to spend some time learning the basics that you will need to know to get started with Arduino. To begin, there are two essentials that you will need; the software to make this work, and the Arduino board.

Understanding the Arduino board

Before you go out and purchase an Arduino board, you will need to understand some of the basic features of these boards and their uses.

There are a few types of boards that are available, and each of them have different capabilities and benefits. While they will differ in terms of what they are able to do and how they look, most of the boards you come across will have the following components in common:

- Barrel Jack and USB - all the boards will have some method for you to connect them to a power source. Most of them will come with a USB connection so that you can upload your codes onto them. You can also choose to connect them with a barrel jack which will essentially let you plug the board into the wall.

- Pins - the pins are where you are going to construct your circuits by connecting in the wires. There are a few types of pins that you can use on the boards and they are each used for a specific function. Some of the most common pins that you will find include:

    o GND: this is short for Gourd. They are the pins that you will use in order to ground your circuit.

    o 5v and 3.3V: these are the pins that will supply either 5 volts or 3.3 Volts of power.

    o Analog: these are the pins that will be seen under the 'Analog In' label. These are the ones that you can use for reading signals from the analog sensors, and then these signals are going to be converted into a digital value.

- Digital: these are going to be across from the analog pins and will be under the 'Digital' label. These are the pins that are used for the input and output of the digital signal.

- PWM: in many of the Arduino boards, there will be a (PWM~) label that is next to the Digital one. This basically means that the pins are able to be used as either normal digital pins, or for a signal that is called Pulse-Width Modulation.

- AREF: this is short form for Analog Reference. This is the pin that you can use to set the upper limit of the external voltage for the analog pins, usually between 0 and 5 volts, though it is often left alone.

- Reset button - this button should be there to allow the pin to rest to the ground, and to restart the code that is already loaded on the board. It is a good way to test out code a few times. It will not reset everything to a clean state, and won't fix any problems that exist in your code.

- Power LED Indicator - this should be a tiny LED light that should have the word "ON" right next to it. It is going to light up when you plug your board into a power source.

- Transmit and Receive LEDs - these are in place to give an indication that the board is either receiving or transmitting data. This is useful when you are trying to load up a new program to the board and you want to see if it is being received.

- Main Integrated Circuit (IC) - this is a little black piece that has metal legs that will attach to the board. Think of it as the brains of the board. The IC will differ between boards, but most are from the ATMEL company. Make sure to know which kind of IC you are using before loading up a new program though because this sometimes does make a difference.

Voltage regulator - this is the component of the board that is going to control how much voltage is able to get onto the board. It has the ability to turn away any extra voltage that is trying to get into the board. It is not able to handle anything that is more than 20 Volts though, so make sure to not use a power supply higher than this or it will destroy the board.

In addition to picking the right board for your project, you need to consider the other hardware that you may want to add on. The board can do a lot of stuff on its own, but it gets a lot of the power you are looking for when you add on some additional hardware. For the basics that we will be learning, it is not such a big deal, but as you progress you may want to consider adding on additional components to get a bit more power.

Getting the software hooked up

After you have had some time to go through and pick out the hardware that you would like to use, including the board you want for the project, it is time to install the IDE for Arduino. This is basically the environment, or the software, that you will need in order to write out the code for the microcontroller and to attach all the circuit components. Without the IDE in place, you would not be able to write out the code and the microcontroller and board would have no idea what you want them to do.

To start, you simply need to visit the Arduino website at www.arduino.cc in order to download the IDE. The IDE will download as a receive a zip folder. Open this up and then save it in a location on your computer that is easy for you to remember.

Once that's done, you will need to run the Arduino.EXE file so that the installation can get started. You simply need to follow the command prompts that come up in order to get everything installed. Once the IDE is set up and you have all the right hardware components, you are ready to move onto the next step of using this programming language!

Chapter 1 Choosing and Setting Up the Arduino

The first step in setting up your Arduino microcontroller will be to choose an Arduino board with which you want to work.

Choosing a Board

When looking at the options for Arduino Boards, there are a few factors you will want to consider before making a choice. Before deciding on a board, ask yourself the following questions:

How much power do I need to run the application I have in mind?

You might not know the exact measure of flash memory and processing power that you require for your project, but there is a clear difference between the functioning of a simple nightlight that changes colors and a robotic hand with many moving parts. The latter would require a more robust Arduino microcontroller board, with faster processing, more flash memory, and more SRAM than the more straightforward night light idea.

How many digital and analog pins will I require to have the functionality that I desire?

Again, you don't need to have an extremely specific idea in mind but knowing whether you need more pins or less will have a great effect on which board you choose. If you are going for a simple first project, you could get away with having less digital, PWM, and analog pins, while if you are looking to do something more complex, you will want to consider the boards with a great number of pins in general.

Do I want this to be a wearable device?

There are a few options for wearable devices so, of course, this question will not entirely make the decision for you. It will, however, help narrow down the choices and steer you in a direction, with Lilypads and the Gemma or other comparable technologies being your best options.

Do I want to connect to the Internet of Things? If so, how?

If you want connectivity to the Internet of Things, your work will be made much easier by the YÚN, the Tian, the Ethernet, the Leonardo ETH, or the Industrial 101. These have the capabilities of Ethernet connection as well as Wi-Fi capability so you will be able to connect to a network like the Internet and share data or interact with and control other devices on the Internet of Things.

Getting Started on Arduino IDE

The Arduino Software runs in an environment called IDE. This means that you will either need to download the desktop IDE to code in or code online on the online IDE.

The first way that you might access IDE, downloading the desktop application, has a few options to suit the various devices that you might be using. First, there is the Windows desktop application. You can also access it from a Windows tablet or Windows phone with the Windows application. Next, there is the Macintosh OSX version, which allows IDE to run on Apple laptops and desktops, but not on Apple mobile devices like iPhones and iPads. Finally, there are three options for running Arduino IDE on Linux: the 32-bit, the 64-bit, and the Linux ARM version. If you prefer this option to the web browser option, you will simply need to visit the Arduino IDE site by heading to HTTPS://WWW.ARDUINO.CC/EN/MAIN/Software

There, you can download the appropriate version of desktop IDE. Next, you will run the installation application, click through the options presented, and you should have a running Arduino IDE environment in just a few minutes.

This allows you to access the IDE software from Android devices and Apple mobile devices as well since it is based in a web browser that runs on its own platform rather than on the Android or iOS platforms. You can also run the web browser on various computer types, including Linux, Microsoft Windows, and Apple Macintosh. This will allow you to upload your sketches to the Cloud, that is, to store the information you have coded in a secure location that you can then re-access from another device by connection to the Internet.

Coding a Program for Your Arduino

Next you will write code for a program that you want the Arduino board to run. This allows you to see the entire code at once, allowing for easier debugging, or removing of errors.

Once you write the code, you will want to run it and troubleshoot or debug any errors that you find. You will best be able to do this by applying the coded program to the Arduino board and seeing if it runs.

To do this, you will need to proceed to the next step of uploading your sketch.

Connecting to the Arduino Board

Some of the boards come with built-in USB, mini-USB, or micro-USB ports. Examples would be the Uno and the Leonardo, for the more beginning stages of your Arduino career. Simply insert the appropriate end of the USB cord into your computer and the other end into the particular USB port that is present on the board you possess, and the Arduino IDE software should recognize the type of board it is. If it does not, you can always choose the correct board from a dropdown menu.

Sometimes you will need to use a TKDI cable or a breakout board in order to make the Arduino compatible with your computer. This means you will insert the TKDI into the TKDI port on the Arduino microcontroller board and then connect it either to your computer or to another board. If you connect the TKDI cable to a breakout board, you will do as you did with the USB-compatible boards: insert the appropriate end of the cord to the breakout board and the other end to the computer. Again, the computer's Arduino IDE software program should recognize your Arduino board, but you can always choose from a dropdown menu should it fail to recognize it.

Uploading to the Arduino Board

To upload your sketch, the program you just created in code, you will need to select the correct board and port to which you would like to upload. It should be easy enough to select the correct board, as you simply look for the board title that matches the name of the type of board you are using.

To select the correct serial port, the options you might choose are as follows:

Mac

Use /*dev*/*tty.usbmodem241* for the Uno, Mega256O or Leonardo.

Use /*dev*/*tty.usbserial-1B1* for Duemilanove or earlier Arduino boards.

Use /*dev*/*tty.USA19QW1b1P1.1* for anything else connected by a USB-to-serial adapter.

Windows

Use *COM1* or *COM2* for a serial board.

Use *COM4*, *COM5*, or *COM7* or higher for a USB-connected board.

Look in Windows Device Manager to determine which port the device you are using is utilizing.

Linux

Use /*dev*/*ttyACMx* for a serial port.

Use /*dev*/*ttyUSBx* or something like it for a USB port.

Once you have selected the correct board and port, click *Upload* and choose which Sketch to upload from the menu that appears. If you have a newer Arduino board, you will be able to upload the new sketch simply, but with the older boards, you must reset the board before uploading a new sketch, else you will have two, possibly conflicting sketches present in the board's memory, causing it to crash.

Running the Arduino with Your Program

There are a few ways to power your Arduino once you have uploaded the program that you have coded to it. First, you can power it by the USB connection to another powered device, such as your computer. Second, you can power by Ethernet on boards with that capability. This means that by connecting to the network, you will be connected to a power source through the Ethernet. Finally, you can power most Arduino's by lithium polymer battery.

Once power is connected, and the specified input is put into the microcontroller, it will perform the function for which it is intended.

Chapter 2 Inputs and Outputs

If you look at the pins on the Arduino panel, you will see that they can be configured as an input or an output. You should remember that a lot of the analog pins have the possibility of needing to be set and used in the same way that a digital pin is going to be used.

Input Pin Configuration

The pins are going to be set to input by default; therefore, they do not need to be declared as an input by using the pinmode ( ) function whenever you want to use them as a contribution. The pins that are configured this way will be in a state of high impedance due to the fact that the input pins are only going to be made to make small demands on the circuit that they sample, which is going to be equal to the series resistor of a hundred megaohm for the front pin.

In other words, it is not going to take much current to switch the input from one state to the next which makes it useful for things like when you need to implement a touch sensor or when you are reading an LED as a photodiode.

The pins that are configured as pinmode will have nothing that is connected to them, if wires are connected to them, then they cannot be attached to another circuit. It has been reported that there are changes in the pins state, environmental commotion picked up through the pins or the capacitive coupling in the situation of a pin that is near the first pin.

Pull Up Resistors

The pull-up resistor is going to be useful when you need to steer the input of a pin to a known state, but you do not have any data present. This is going to be best when there is no input. All you need to do is add a pull-up resistor that goes up to 5 volts, or you can choose a pull-down resistor for the input. It is best that you use a 10k resistor that is going to be good for pulling up or pulling down the resistor.

Using the Built-In Pull-Up Resistor with the Pins Configured to Input

In the Atmega chip, there are around 20,000 pull-up resistors that are built into it that you are going to have access to in the software. These resistors are going to be accessed through your pinmod () setting by inputting input_pullup. Now you have inverted the behavior of your contribution mode so that high will turn the sensor off and low will turn the sensor on.

The various values for the pull-up are going to depend on what kind of microcontroller you are using. For many AVR panels, the value is going to be between 20 and 50 k ohms. For the Arduino Due, you will find that it is between 50k and 150 k ohms. To figure out what the exact value is, you will need to look at the datasheet for the microcontroller that is installed on your panel.

Whenever you connect sensors to the pins that are configured for input, you need to ensure that the other end is grounded. This is done so that if the pin is reading high, the switch is going to be opened and little means that the switch is pressed. With pull-up resistors, you are going to be able to provide enough current to light up the LED that is connected to the pin.

There are some registers that are going to tell the pin if it is on a high or low while controlling the pull-up resistor. There are also pins that can be configured to have the pull-up resistor turned on whenever the pin is in input mode, which will mean that the pin is turned on to high. Should the pin be switched over to output by use of the pinmode () function, then it is going to work the opposite direction. So, if the pin is on output mode, the high state is going to have the resistor set up to where if switched it will go into input mode.

Example

pinmode (4, input) ; // the pin is set to input

pinmode (6, input_pullup) ;

Pins Configured To Output

Any pin capable of configuration will do so to output with pinmode ( ) and will be the lower state of impedance. With that being said, they are going to be able to provide a large amount of current to other circuits that are hooked up to it. The Atmega pins are going to give you the positive current or the negative current depending on how many milliamps of current the other pieces of equipment are going to need. As long as it is 40 mA or under, you will be able to have enough current to light up an LED brightly, but it is not going to be enough to run any motors.

Whenever you attempt to run a device that is going to require a lot of currents, the pins can become damaged or even destroyed. This can end up destroying the entire Atmega chip which is going to result in a dead pin in your microcontroller. However, the other pins are going to work still, but they may work at a lesser power than they were before. That is why you should hook your output pins up to another device that is either 470 ohms or is a 1k resistor. The only time that you should not is if the current draw that is coming from the pins is required to run a certain application.

Pinmode () function

Pin mode is going to be used whenever you are configuring a specific pin so that it is going to behave as an input or an output pin. There is the possibility that you can enable the internal pull-up resistor through the input_pullup mode. It also makes it to where the input mode is going to disable any internal pull-ups.

Syntax:

Void setup () {

Pinmode (pin, mode) ;

}

1. Pin is going to be the digital representation of pins that you want to set the mode for.

Mode will be either input, output, or input_pullup.

Digitalwrite ( ) function

This is a super function that you can use when you need to write the code containing higher or lower values for the personal digital pin previously setup. Should the pin be configured for output, then the voltage needs to be set to the value of 5 volts. There cannot be any volts for low because it will need to be grounded.

If the pin is on input, then the high setting is going to be disabled while the low is going to be the pullup internally for the pin. We strongly advise that you setup your personal pinmode ( ) function so that input_pullup. Otherwise, it might not be able to pull up the resistor interior of the panel.

If you do not set the pin mode for output and then proceed to connect an LED tot hat pin as you call on the high setting, then the LED is going to appear dimmer than it should be. If you do not explicitly set the pin mode and digital write functions to enable the internal pullup, it is going to do so automatically which is going to act as a massive current capable of limiting the resistor.

Syntax

Void loop ( ) {

digitalWrite (pin, value) ;

}

1. Pin is going to be the digital representation of pins that you want to set to input or output.

Value is the high or low setting.

Analogread ( ) function

The Arduino program is capable of detection of all levels. Here, it can determine whether or not there is voltage, perhaps inadvertently, finding itself applied to one of the pins before it sends the report back through the digitalread ( ) function. You have to know that there is a difference between the on and off sensor so that the analog sensor is constantly charging. To read this type of sensor, you are going to require a different type of pin.

When you look at the lower right of your panel, there are going to be six pins that are marked as analog in. These pins are not just going to tell if there is any voltage being applied to them, but also how much is flowing through it. When you use the analogread ( ) function, you will be able to read the voltage that is applied to just one of the pins.

For this function, a digital representation is going to be returned between 0 and 1023 to represent the voltage between 0 and 5 volts. An example would be if you have a voltage of 2.5 V that is being applied to the pin digital representation 3, you will get a return of 512.

Syntax

Analogread (pin) ;

Pin: the digital representation of which pin to be read from 0 to 5 on a great majority of panels. 0 to 7 if you are using the mini and Nano panels. And then 0 to 15 on the Mega panels.

Vertical Integration Projects

Project 5: Transmitter and Receiver Arduinos Description

The term i2c is pronounced "I" squared "C" which is protocol that allows multiple devices to interact on a two-wire bus. In this case one Arduino is described as the transmitter (TX). The second Arduino is designated the receiving Arduino (RX). The TX Arduino is the control panel with a switch and two LEDs. The lighted LED shows which route is selected. The second Arduino receives control inputs regarding route selection, which it uses to control two servos attached to two turnouts. Each servo is mounted to a turnout, which is located at the end of a passing track. The second Arduino has one LED that lights up when Route B is selected.

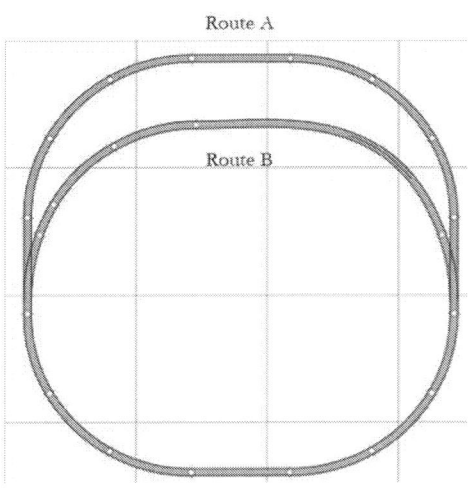

Figure 36: Route A and B on Demonstration Layout
Material

The material needed for this dual Arduino system includes:
- 2 Arduinos UNO
- Switch
- Multiple LEDs
- 2 servos
- 2 Atlas HO scale "snap" turnouts
- For mounting the servo to the turnout: miscellaneous screws, styrene, wood
- For wiring to the turnout servos: wires, terminal blocks, and cable ties

Challenge

The challenge in this project was getting the two Arduinos communicating, after the authors and others tried several techniques they developed these versions of the TX and RX code in this chapter that work very well.

Diagrams

This project uses Atlas snap turnouts, which have a couple of mounting holes. The figure shows how the servo is mounted to the Atlas turnout. Using a small piece of styrene, a hole is drilled and tapped at one end, and this attaches to the turnout. A second hole is drilled and tapped on the side of the styrene. This is how the servo is mounted to the styrene. Next a small block of wood with a "v" notch filed into it provides the yoke that the servo interfaces with, using a small screw attached to the servo arm. This provides the model railroader with a nicely integrated package. With a few servo rotation tweaks, it will not need to be adjusted. The authors found that setting up turnouts under layout was a challenge. The setup described here allows the minor tweaks to be done above the layout, and then the turnout is installed on the layout with no adjustments needed.

Physical Integration of Servo on Atlas Turnout

The following schematics show how the two Arduinos are connected together. The first schematic shows how the TX Arduino is connected to the LED. The second schematic indicates how to connect the Arduino to the servos on the turnouts.

LED Route A
GND

LED Route B
GND

SDA on
Other
ArduinoSCL on

Other Arduino
Computer Port
Digital
Processor
Chip
OutputAnalogPower
Power

Ground on
Other Arduino

5 V on Other Arduino

Transmitter Arduino with Two LEDs Indicating which Route is Selected
Servo 1 5 volt **+5V**
Ground **GND** Signal
GND
+5V 5 volt
Ground **Servo 2** Signal

LED

SDA on Other
Arduino SCL on Other
Arduino GND

Computer Port
Digital
4.7 K 4.7 K Processor Chip
Battery Power Sensor Power Analog

Ground on
Other
Arduino
Ground on
Servos

5 V on Other Arduino 5 V on

Servos

Receiver Arduino with Servos on Two Turnouts

Note: The authors determined the power should be provided to the RX

Arduino otherwise there was not enough power to operate the servos.

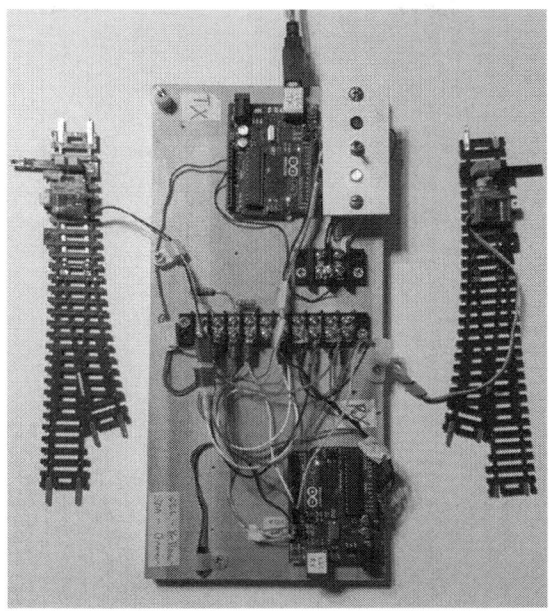

TX and RX Arduinos with Control Panel

Transmitter Arduino Code

The goal of this code is for the TX Arduino to transmit the command from a switch to the RX Arduino. It also lights one of two LEDs on the control panel, depending on which route is selected.

// The original code was based:
// I2C Master
// By Cornel Amariei for Packt Publishing

```
//https://www.instructables.com/id/I2C-Between-Arduinos-With-Potentiometer-and-LED/

// i2c_TX_12_23_18 Modified by Fitz Walker, Paul Bradt and David Bradt
//This version works great sends signal to RX and lights LEDs
#include <Wire.h>
const int BUTTON = 4;

int x = 1; //Initialize switch state
int redLED = 7; //connect red LED to pin 7 int greenLED = 6;
//connect green LED to pin 6

void setup() {
// Start the I2C Bus as Master
Wire.begin();
pinMode(BUTTON, INPUT_PULLUP); //Setup switch with internal pullup resistor pinMode(redLED, OUTPUT); //setup LED
pinMode(greenLED, OUTPUT); //setup LED
Serial.begin(9600);

}
void loop() {
x = digitalRead(BUTTON); //Read switch input

if (x == LOW) {
Wire.beginTransmission(9); // transmit Swtich state x to device #9 RX Arduino digitalWrite(redLED, HIGH);
```

```
digitalWrite(greenLED, LOW);
Wire.write(x);
Wire.endTransmission(); // stop transmitting
Serial.print("Button State: "); // Use for trouble shooting
Serial.println(x); //Send switch state to Serial Port
delay(2000);

}

if (x == HIGH) {
Wire.beginTransmission(9); // transmit Swtich state x to device #9 RX Arduino
digitalWrite(redLED, LOW);
digitalWrite(greenLED, HIGH);
Wire.write(x);
Wire.endTransmission(); // stop transmitting
Serial.print("Button State: "); // Use for trouble shooting
Serial.println(x); //Send switch state to Serial Port
delay(2000);

}
}
```

Receiver Arduino Code

After getting a command from the TX Arduino, the RX Arduino controls two turnouts so they operate together for selecting a route on a passing track. It also lights an LED which is located near the turnouts for local indication of route selection.

```
// The original code was based:
// I2C Slave
// By Cornel Amariei for Packt Publishing
//https://www.instructables.com/id/I2C-Between-Arduinos-With-Potentiometer-and-LED/

// i2c_RX_12_23_2018 Modified extensively by Fitz Walker, Paul Bradt and David Bradt //Compiles LED lights up on RX Arduino(Device # 9) and Servo increments, //returns after switch returned
//Data shows up serial bus when Switch thrown on TX Arduino
//Power from RX Arduino

#include <Wire.h>  //Start wire library #include <Servo.h>  //Start Servo library

int LED = 13; //Setup onboard LED int LED2 = 7; //Attach LED
int x = 0; //Initialize Variable sent from TX

Servo turnOut1; //Setup Servo on turnOut1 Servo turnOut2; //Setup Servo on turnOut2

void setup() {
  // Define the LED pin as Output
```

```
pinMode (LED, OUTPUT);
pinMode (LED2, OUTPUT);
turnOut1.attach(9); //Attach turnOut1 servo to pin 9
turnOut2.attach(11); //Attach turnOut2 servo to pin 11

// Start the I2C Bus as Slave on address for Device #9 RX Arduino
Wire.begin(9);
// Attach a function to trigger when something is received.
Wire.onReceive(receiveEvent);
Serial.begin(9600);

}
void receiveEvent(int bytes) {
x = Wire.read(); // read one character from the I2C sent from TX Arduino Serial.print(x);

if (x == 1) {
digitalWrite(LED2, HIGH);
digitalWrite(LED, HIGH);
turnOut1.write(60); //Adjust this for turnout throw turnOut2.write(60);
//Adjust this for turnout throw delay(2000);

}

if(x == 0) {
digitalWrite(LED2, LOW);
digitalWrite(LED, LOW);
```

```
turnOut1.write(80); //Adjust this for turnout throw turnOut2.write(80);
//Adjust this for turnout throw delay(2000);

    }
}
void loop() {
}
```

Operation

The operation of this two-Arduino system is completed by simply flipping a switch that lights a specific LED along with sending a signal to the second Arduino, which activates two solenoids that position the turnouts to the proper route.

Summary

This project demonstrates the use of one Arduino as a control device and a second Arduino as an effector, operating two servos simultaneously switching the route from one direction to the second direction. The operations in this project could easily be combined on one Arduino. The authors purposely structured this project to demonstrate a vertically integrated system that shows the reader the possibility of separating functions on more than one Arduino.

Project 6: JMRI Interface to Arduino

Description

Project 6 uses JAVA Model Railroad Interface (JMRI) to control an Arduino that positions turnouts to the proper route on the layout. JMRI is an incredibly versatile tool that is well suited to controlling many aspects of large layouts. This system uses vertical integration of a computer running JMRI, which sends the signal to the local Arduino, which in turn activates two solenoids that control the turnouts so they move to the proper route configuration.

JMRI is a complex, powerful program, and this book only scratches the surface of its capabilities and highlights one small use for it. If the reader is interested in finding out how to use JMRI, the authors recommend finding an online JMRI group such as *jmriusers@groups.io*, or someone local that is familiar with the program and its features. For this book we are utilizing the Panel Pro section in JMRI and the ability to send commands to a remote effector.

With the proper setup, JMRI could do this on its own without an Arduino, but the authors wanted to develop and implement this solution to demonstrate another way to perform the function.

Material

The material needed for this project:
- Arduino UNO
- 2 servos
- 2 Atlas turnouts

53

- Miscellaneous screws, styrene, and wood for mounting the servo to the turnout
- Wires, terminal blocks, and cable ties for the wiring to the turnouts
- JMRI loaded on the computer
- Computer Model Railroad Interface (CMRI) and Auto485 libraries download for the code
- Modified Iron Ridge Station kit (Walthers: 931-904)

The only modification to the building is that the opening underneath needs to be expanded.

Diagrams

The following diagrams show the setup of the JMRI Arduino.

Arduino Set Up to Work with JMRI

Servo 1 Servo 2 +5V 5 volt 5 volt +5V GND Ground Ground GND
Signal Signal
Computer DIGITAL Port
Processor Chip

SENSOR ANALOGBatteryPOWER

Power

+5V

GND

Schematic for Two Servos on Turnout

Challenges

Connecting the Arduino to the computer and having JMRI operate it to position two turnouts is a significant challenge. JMRI is a little tricky to get working. The following steps, shown here and on the website, should help the user work through these challenges.

Operations and JMRI Setup

The link to the JMRI website is shown below. The website provides a good introductory tutorial for learning the basics of setup and control of both the JMRI and the Arduino.

http://www.motorhomesites.org.uk/jmri-arduino-setup/

The general steps to follow are:

Load JMRI from the following location on to a computer.

http://jmri.sourceforge.net/

Load the CMRI library from the site below.

https://github.com/madleech/ArduinoCMRI

Refer to the library at the site below.

- Start Panel Pro
  - Configure the node for Arduino based on the com port it is in

- Open up tables and configure the servos on the turnouts
- Load the Arduino code below
- Restart JMRI and select the turnouts.

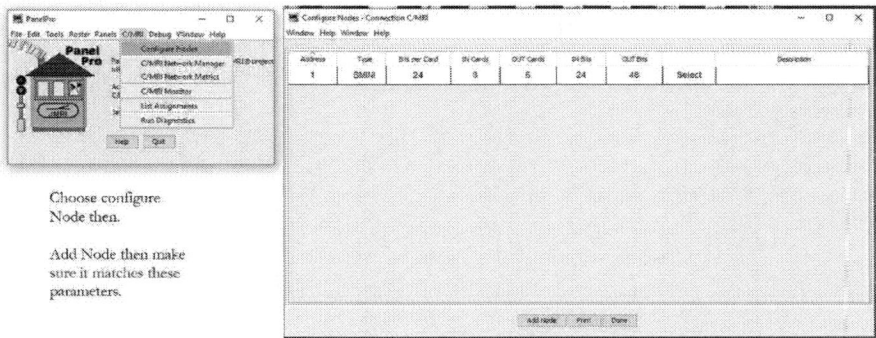

Choose configure Node then.

Add Node then make sure it matches these parameters.

Setup and Configuring Nodes

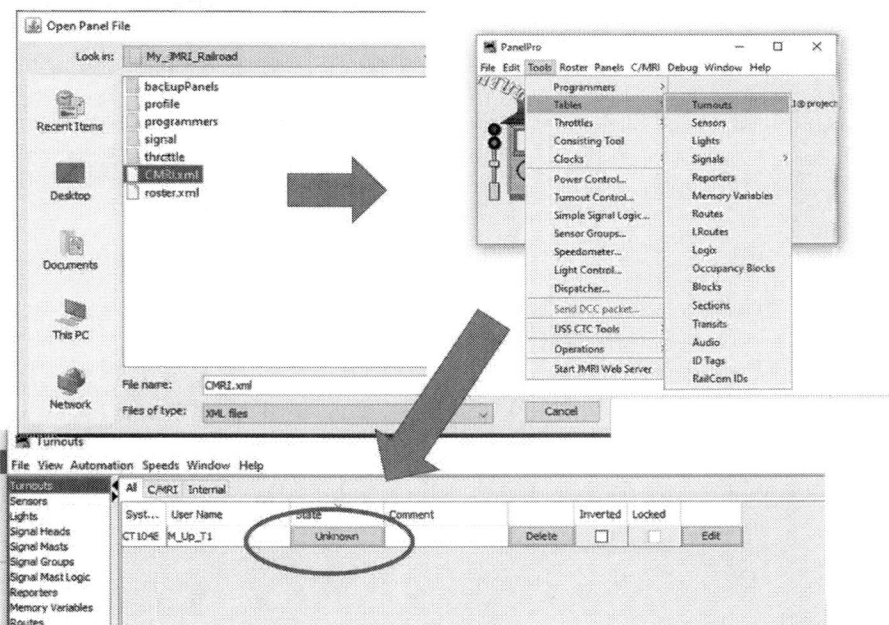

Selecting Control Panel Created and Turnout

57

If the reader is new to JMRI, the authors recommend walking through all of the tutorials on the site referenced [11]. As noted above, it is a very good introduction to the basics of JMRI and how to recognize and control an Arduino. The website is an excellent reference, but the authors did find one thing that was not needed for our setup. On the website the author indicated the need to rotate the servo back slightly after moving to one position. This part of the code actually caused our servos to hunt and chitter. After removing that part of the code it worked perfectly.

Arduino Code

//SN019 11_15_2018 modified by Paul Bradt and David Bradt code from this site: //http://www.motorhomesites.org.uk/jmri-arduino-turnout-setup/

#include <CMRI.h> //include CMRI library #include <Auto485.h> //include Auto485b library #include <Servo.h> // include servo library

#define CMRI_ADDR 1 //Define CMRI Address
#define DE_PIN 2 //Define serial connection via Auto485 bus
int turnout1 = 0; int turnout2 = 0;

Auto485 bus(DE_PIN); // Arduino pin 2 -> MAX485 DE and RE pins
CMRI cmri(CMRI_ADDR, 24, 48, bus);

```
// defaults to a SMINI with address 0. SMINI = 24 inputs, 48 outputs
and uses Auto485's bus

Servo turnOut1; Servo turnOut2;

void setup() {
//Setup turnOut and bus turnOut1.attach(9);
turnOut1.write(4);
turnOut2.attach(8);
turnOut2.write(6);
bus.begin(9600);

}
void loop() {
//Starting cmri each time loop runs cmri.process();

//Checking out cmri bit 47 and run motor for both turnOut 1 and 2
turnout1 = (cmri.get_bit(47));
if (turnout1 == 1) {

turnOut1.write(36); //Adjust turnout throw if needed }
else {

turnOut1.write(4); //Adjust turnout throw if needed
}
turnout2 = (cmri.get_bit(47));
if (turnout2 == 1) {
turnOut2.write(50); //Adjust turnout throw if needed
}
```

```
else {
turnOut2.write(6); //Adjust turnout throw if needed

}
}
```

It should be noted that the JMRI only sees this as one turnout, because the Arduino is controlling both turnouts with one input from JMRI. Once the setup is configured and working, when it is restarted only four steps are needed, but they must be completed in this order:

Step 1: Connect the Arduino to the exact same USB port on the computer as when it was initially set up.

Step 2: Open Panel Pro

Step 3: Open the Panel that was previously configured.

Step 4: Open the Turnout Table that was previously configured.

It is ready to operate!

Summary

JMRI is a powerful tool and has a number of other capabilities which can seem overwhelming to the novice. The website identified and the information in this chapter provide excellent step-by-step guidance on how to set up and control an Arduino with JMRI. The authors hope the experience shared and the reference website encourage the model railroader to try to use JMRI.

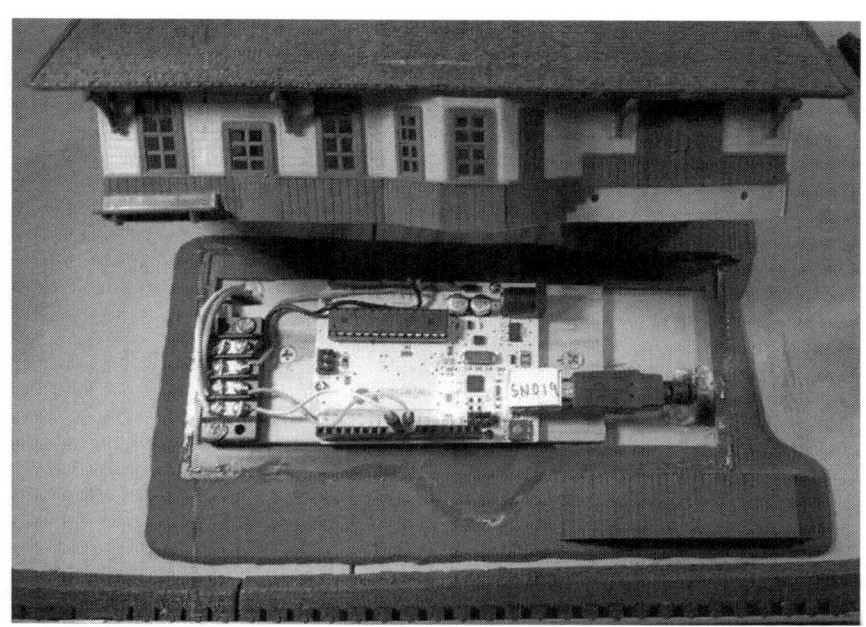

JMRI Arduino Inside Station

Chapter 3 Modulating the On-Board LED and Persistence of Vision

In our blink sketch, we manipulated the on-board LED in the most basic and simple way: we turned it off and on with the same delay.

In our *It's Alive* sketch, we manipulated the on and off times and changed the pattern.

This demonstrated the basic structure of a sketch to control the LED to make any pattern we want.

In this experiment, we will write a sketch which will turn the LED off and on to generate a simple pulse train. This is one of the basic building block signals we will use over and over again.

What you need to know and what you will learn in this experiment

You should be comfortable using the following commands:

void setup()

PINMODE(13, OUTPUT);

void loop() {

DIGITALWRITE(13, HIGH);

DELAY(100);

Serial.begin(9600);

Serial.PRINT("Hello World");

Serial.PRINTLN(" ");

//comments

In this chapter, we will introduce a valuable feature: variables, their care and feeding. Every sketch we use going forward will use variables. This will introduce you to the abstract thinking of algebra and the essence of programming.

The basic pulse train pattern

A pulse train is a repeating pattern of on and offs. We can describe this pattern with a few *figures of merit*. A figure of merit is a number that characterizes a behavior. It is based on using an ideal pattern as a template with the figures of merit describing specific features. We compare our signal to the template and what value of figure of merit makes the ideal signal match our actual signal.

For example, to describe a pulse train of on's and off's, we could use:

- *On-time*
- *Off-time*
- *Off-voltage (low)*
- *On-voltage (high)*

The generic structure of this ideal pulse train, identifying the figures of

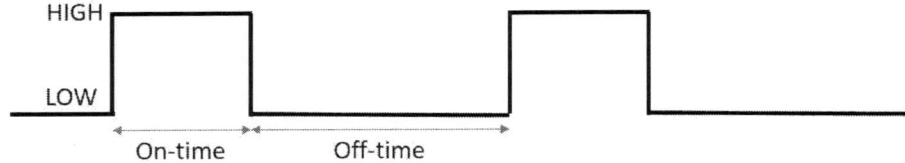

merit, is shown in *Figure 5.32*.

Example of a simple pulse train of repeating on-time, off-time, on-time, off-time pulses.

This is exactly the structure of the Blink sketch. We can literally use it and just adjust the on-time and the off-time. Here is how we would use it:

void setup() {

   PINMODE(13, OUTPUT);

}

void loop() {

   DIGITALWRITE(13, HIGH);

   DELAY(1000); // on time

   DIGITALWRITE(13, LOW);

   DELAY(1000); //off time

}

This is a great opportunity for you to get your sense of short time intervals calibrated.

Try this experiment: Set the on-time and off-time to be 1000 msec and get familiar with what this time interval feels like. This will give you a calibrated 1 second interval (the on-time) with which to get comfortable.

Then, try this with a 500 msec on-time. Can you train your eye to judge how long ½ a second is?

What is the flicker rate?

As written, the sketch in the last section will modulate the LED with the same on and off time. Using this pattern, we can explore the questions of how fast we can modulate the LED so that it appears to be continuously on.

As we decrease the off and on time, we reach a point where the LED looks like it is no longer blinking, but on continuously. We call this rate the flicker rate.

We already introduced one set of figures of merit that describe this pulse train, the on and off times. We can describe this behavior with another set of parameters or figures of merit.

This is a *periodic* behavior. The same pattern of on and off lights happens over and over again. We call one complete pattern a *cycle*.

One term that describes a property of a cycle is the time it takes to complete. This is called the *period*. If the on-time is 0.5 seconds and the off-time is 0.5 seconds, the period is the total time for one cycle or 1 second per cycle.

An alternative way of describing the properties of a cycle is its *frequency*, how many cycles are completed per second. The frequency of a periodic event is also referred to as a *rate* or *speed*. These terms are a little ambiguous. The *frequency* of the pattern is a better term to always use.

If we know the period per cycle, the frequency is how many cycles occur per second. The frequency is the inverse of the period:

If the period uses units of seconds per cycle, the units of frequency are cycles per second. For historical reasons, we call cycles per second, Hertz, abbreviated Hz.

The flicker rate, or flicker frequency, is the lowest frequency at which the LED appears to be on continuously. At a slightly lower frequency, the LED will appear to noticeably flicker. A higher frequency than the flicker rate and the LED will appear to be on continuously.

To calculate the flicker rate, first decrease the off and on time until the LED appears to not be blinking. The total time, the off-time + the on-time = the *period* of the pulse train. The flicker frequency is

For example, when I adjusted the on and off time, I found that when the on and off time was each 20 msec, the LED appeared to be on continuously. The period was 40 msec = 0.04 sec and the flicker frequency was 1/0.04 sec = 25 Hz.

This is close to the value of 24 frames per second (fps), which is the frame rate used in movies. Why 24 fps? A slower rate and there is perception of individual frames. A faster rate and you use up more film. To reduce the cost of the film, the absolutely lowest rate that is still flicker free was selected. For historical reason, 24 fps was adopted. You can *read about it here*.

Here is my sketch to drive the on-board LED at 25 Hz:

```
void setup() {
    PINMODE(13, OUTPUT);
}

void loop() {
    DIGITALWRITE(13, HIGH);
    DELAY(20); // on time
    DIGITALWRITE(13, LOW);
    DELAY(20); //off time
}
```

If we pulse the LED at a rate slower than 25 Hz, we can see the LED is flashing. If it is faster than 25 Hz, the flashes blur together in the after image in our eye and it looks continuously on.

Try this experiment: Use the Blink sketch to measure the flicker rate for you and your friends.

In many cars, the red lights used for brake lights or the back lights when the headlights are on, use red LEDs. These are often flashing off and on, but at a rate faster than most peoples' flicker rate.

The way to tell if a car's lights are actually flashing is to move your eyes rapidly around. Your peripheral vision will pick up the lights as streaks. If the light is really being flashed on and off, the streaks will have dashes in them.

When I drive at night, I sometimes move my eyes rapidly side to side when I look at a car's back lights. When I see short dashes in the afterimage, I can tell the car lights are LEDs and they are being modulated.

Changing the apparent brightness

If we use a total period that is shorter than the flicker period, the LED will appear to be on continuously. The persistence of vision in our eyes keeps a little of the image of the on-LED in our vision even when it is off. It's like our vision has some memory to it. The LED has to be off for some period of time for us to forget it was ever on and see it as an off.

To pulse the LED so it looks continuously on, we need to keep the sum of the on and off times shorter than 40 msec.

We can change the apparent brightness of the LED if we make the fraction of time the LED is on shorter or longer.

If we use an on-time of 40 msec, and off-time of 0 msec, the LED will always be on and it will look the brightest.

If the on-time is 20 msec and the off-time 20 msec, the brightness will look mid-range.

If the on-time is 1 msec and the off-time is 39 msec, the LED will look very dim.

Try these experiments:

1. Modulate the LED at the three different brightness levels and compare their relative brightness. Since the fraction of time the LED is on is very precisely controlled, the relative brightness is very linear.

2. This is a chance to calibrate your eye. Does the sensation of brightness match what you set?

3. As you move your eyes around quickly, do you see the length of the LED streak change length with the on-time?

The *apparent* brightness is really related to the *fraction* of the *whole time interval* in which the LED is on. The larger the fraction of time the LED is on in one cycle, the brighter it will look.

We call the fraction of time the LED is on, the *duty cycle*. When the duty cycle is 100%, the LED will be the brightest. When the duty cycle is 50%, it will be dimmer, and when the duty cycle is 2.5%, with the on-time 1 msec out of a total interval of 40 msec, (1/40 = 2.5%), it will be dimmest, before it is finally off.

Try different duty cycles and see if you can calibrate your sensation of brightness with duty cycle.

New Features: Introducing variables and variable types

So far, when we wanted to identify a specific pin, or we wanted a specific delay time, we typed the specific number into the sketch. We call this *hard coding* the number. Every time we wanted to change that number, we had to go in and type a new number. This worked but it was very rigid and awkward. By using *variables*, we dramatically simplify coding.

Variables are names we give to parameters that will hold the value of a number or character. They are a symbolic placeholder for some set of data. We can use the variable name to replace the number or characters in any calculation or operation.

In computer-speak jargon, the *variable* name is the name of the location in memory in which we store the value of the data. Whenever we use the variable name, it points to the data stored in that location.

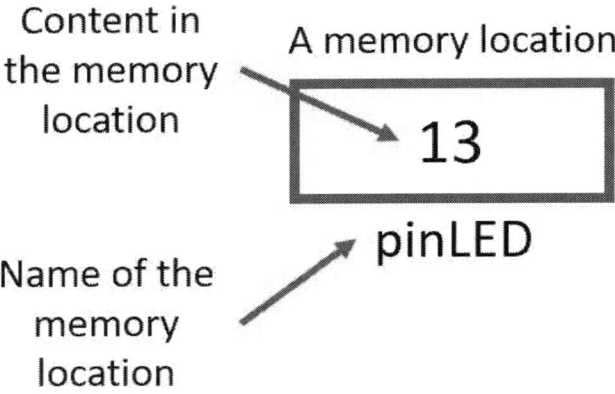

How to think of a variable as a location in memory that stores a number.

In the Blink sketch, pin 13 is the pin to which the on-board LED is connected. We *hard-coded* the number 13 by typing it explicitly in the DIGITALWRITE command. We could have given the on-board pin number a variable name, or memory location label, such as the made-up name, pinLED.

We tell the sketch *pinLED* is a variable and create the variable location by declaring it at the very beginning of the sketch using a special syntax. At the same time we declare the variable, which creates it, we can also place in its memory location the number 13.

At any future time, we could refer to the pin number by this variable name and write the command, for example, as

DIGITALWRITE (pinLED, HIGH);

In every command in which we need to address pin 13, we could use its variable name, pinLED. Whatever command sees the variable name pinLED will look up in its memory location the value stored there and use this value. If we later decide to use pin 12 instead, we just change the value of the number stored in the pinLED variable name location and pin 12 is used everywhere.

Every variable has three elements:

- *a type*
- *a name*
- *a value*

The *name* and *value* we described above. There are multiple types of variables based on what sort of data is stored in its location, such as: *int, long, float, Boolean, string, char,* and *arrays*.

In most of the sketches we will write, we will use two types of numbers: *integers* (a whole number with a plus or minus sign) like 448, 12, -94 or -5, and numbers with a decimal point, we call *floating point* numbers, like 4.81 or -2456.12.

The difference between an integer and a floating point number is that a floating point number has a decimal point, but an integer does not.

When we create a *variable* we want to use to represent a number, we have to decide, when we create it, if we want the number to be an *integer* or a *floating-point* number. The *number type* influences the sort of math we do with it and how the variable can be used.

For example, if we want to use the variable as a pin number, it must be an *integer* type. We create integer type numbers using the simple command

int pinLED;

Some functions, like delay() will only use integers. However, if you type a delay of 145.57 inside the (), the delay function will turn it into an *integer* by truncating everything after the decimal point.

If we want to use the variable in a delay function as a delay of some number of milliseconds, it is a good habit to use a number that is an *integer* type. This way, we know exactly what delay value will be used.

The value of a number created from reading an analog pin is an *integer* type.

An *integer* type number has no decimal point. It is only a whole number. If we try to assign a number like 15.3 to a variable we created as an integer variable, only the whole part of the number, 15, will be stored in the variable location.

This means that when we do some algebra like 5/2 and assign the value to a variable that is an integer type, only the integer part of the answer will be stored.

Sometimes, this is a useful feature, such as when we want an answer as a whole number. Sometimes this results in a number we did not want, like when we are taking an average and the average is less than 1. If assigned to an integer variable, its value would be 0.

There are some limitations to the variable type "int". A variable defined as an *int* can only have a value between -32,768 to 32,767.

This is not a very large range. If we use an int variable to count milliseconds, the longest amount of time we can count is only 32.7 seconds.

If the value of our variable is already 32,767 and we add 1 to it, it rolls over to -32768 and counts up from there. This could be very inconvenient if we don't plan for it.

There will be many situations in which we want larger integer values. In this case, there is a different type of integer we can create, called a *long*. Instead of using the *int* command to declare an integer, we use the long command and declare a long integer. The command looks like:

long iCount;

A long variable can be between -2,147,483,648 to 2,147,483,647. If we use a long type variable to count milliseconds, we could count as many as 2 million seconds, which is about 1 ½ months.

You can never go wrong creating all your integer variable types as long. It will take up a little bit more memory space, but if memory is ever a problem, there are other microcontrollers you can switch over to where memory is not a limitation. They will not be the lowest cost, but they will still be low cost, and higher performance.

We create a variable in the beginning of a sketch before the void setup() function. The syntax is the type of variable and the variable name. We can include an initial value if we want. Here are a few examples:

int iCounter=0;

long iTime_msec=17;

float V_tempSensor_V;

Try these experiments:

1. Any number assigned to an integer will always be in the format of an integer. What will int i1= 3.1415 be? Try creating the variable, assigning it this value and printing the variable to the serial monitor.

2. The largest integer you can store is 32,767. if you try to make an integer with a value of 32,768, it will roll over to the very beginning and start up. What value is i1=32768 or higher?

3. If you declare the integer as a long, you can count larger integers. What is long i1=40000, compared to int i2=40000?

4. When we declare a variable at the beginning of a sketch, we can:

a. just declare the memory space, int i3

b. declare the memory space and set a value to the variable, int i3 = 12

c. declare the memory space, and perform a simple calculation using other, previously defined variables. long i4 = i2 + i1

5. What is int i2=14+13.6? What is long i9=329000+29?

Remember, you can print a variable's value to the serial monitor using just a few lines of code, like:

int i1 = 3456;

void setup() {

    Serial.begin(2000000);

}

void loop() {

    Serial.println(i1);

}

Floating-point type numbers are numbers with a decimal point. A *floating-point* type variable cannot be used as a *counter* in an *if* statement or as a *pin* number or in the delay function.

77

However, the *floating-point* type number is incredibly useful when describing a voltage, or a temperature.

Generally, if there is no compelling reason why a number should be an integer, or we think that when we use the variable, it may represent a number with a decimal point, the variable type should be assigned float.

To use a variable, we have to first create it, or in computer jargon, *declare* it, by defining what type of number we want it to be, *integer* or *floating point*. It's a good habit to declare the variable at the beginning of the sketch before the setup() function. The command lines to create an integer or a floating-point variable, labeled as pinLED and sensorVoltage are:

int pinLED;

float sensorVoltage;

The command to declare an integer variable is int.

This command allocates a little space in memory, labeled pinLED, that will store an *integer type* number. At some point in the sketch we need to fill this memory location with the value of the number we want. We can both declare the variable and assign it a value all in the same line, such as with

int pinLED = 13;

In most cases, we place these lines of code which declare the variable and allocate the memory space, at the beginning of the sketch, before the ^{void} **setup()** function. We can change the value of the variable anywhere in the code that is appropriate.

A *floating-point type* number can have a value from 3.4028235E+38 to as low as -3.4028235E+38. Each float has 6 or 7 digits and an exponent. Hopefully, you will not encounter a sketch where you need a bigger number.

Try these experiments (think about what you expect to see before you do it and see if it comes out the way you expect):

1. Create an integer and make it equal to 3200, then print it to the serial port, over and over again.

2. Create a floating point variable equal to 25.991 and print it to the serial monitor.

3. Create a new floating-point variable equal to 22.4 and an integer, equal to 10. Then, assign the integer to equal the floating-point number. Print them both out.

New Features: Variable names

Variables are key elements in every sketch. The hardest part in using variables is thinking of *good names* for them. While we can use almost any name we want, I have certain guidelines that I use based on years of coding in many different languages.

The constraint on variable names is that they can't start with a number and can't have spaces. The only non-letter or number they can use is an underscore, "_".

For example, perfectly good variable names are:

- *a*
- *a5*
- *LED_pin*
- *b4*

In the olden days, with very limited memory in a computer, variable names were restricted to a single letter and a number. It was always a challenge trying to remember was the temperature sensor value variable name T3 or S2?

But these days, even in an Arduino, variable names can be 64 characters long or longer. So how do we design a good variable name?

As a *Best Design Practice*, the goal in selecting a variable name is to keep it short yet encode valuable information so it is self-documenting. Some of the information we could encode in the variable name are:

- *what type of variable: long, float, array, string...*
- *what element of the Arduino it refers: a pin, an input, out,...*
- *what the source or use of the number might be- as a specific sensor input, an LED value, a tone value...*
- *the units of the number stored in the variable*

Good variable names encode the most useful information so that you can remember what they mean a month later, or someone new to the code can decipher what the variable might contain.

If you use a consistent naming approach, your variables will be easy to decipher without having to check in the comment line, easy to remember, and easy to figure out if you don't want to find where it is declared. We want to establish good variable naming habits that are *self-documenting*.

Everyone has a different style when naming *variables*. This makes trying to figure out what is a variable and what type it is, just from the name, can be very confusing when reading someone else's sketch.

Here are two very good descriptions of variable naming conventions:

http://codebuild.blogspot.com/2012/02/15-best-practices-of-variable-method.html

https://dev.to/mohitrajput987/coding-best-practices-part-1-naming-conventions--class-designing-principles

Generally, I like to use variable names that describe the type of variable, in what general and specific context it is used and include the units of the number contained in the variable location.

To describe an integer, I like to start with the letter "i" or "n", like iCounter, or nptsAve_volts.

The rest of the name describes what the variable is used for and ends with the units. Here are some examples:

nCountCycles

iTimeStart_msec

iTimeStop_usec

sensorTemp1_volts

sensorTemp1_degC

iSensorTemp1_ADU

SensorTemp1_ADU

pinTemp1_hi

pinTemp1_lo

Any variable that refers to a pin name is unambiguously an integer, so starting with the word "pin" is ok.

The last part of any variable name is the units of the variable. To highlight the units, I set them off with an underscore, _, at the end of the variable name. If it is a time, the units might be _sec, or _msec, or _usec. If it is a voltage, it might be _volts or just _V or _mV.

In the special case of the levels from an *analog pin*, there are no units. The value is dimensionless. However, to help me keep track that the variable is a number from an analog pin, I use the units of *Analog to Digital Units* or _ADU. I always place the characters "ADU" at the end of a variable name that will store the value read from an analog channel.

Even though a number in units of ADU, the number read from an ADC (Analog to Digital Converter), is an integer, sometimes we will make these float type numbers so we can do more accurate math, like when taking averages.

If the variable is used as a simple index number inside of a loop or in an array, which has meaning only as an index number, I would just use the letter i or i1 or i2 or i3.

There are no hard and fast rules. The Best Design Practice is to use variable names that help to describe what the variable refers to so anyone reading your code would have a clear idea. The second-best approach is to be consistent.

It's important to develop good habits early on so that each sketch is an opportunity to practice and so that all of your projects become *self-documenting*.

You can never add too many comments to further clarify each variable.

Let's practice some of these variable principles.

Try these experiments:

1. What would be a good variable name for the pin driving an LED?

2. What is 20/3?

3. What is 20/3.0?

4. What would be a good variable name for the voltage of a sensor, stored as millivolts?

5. What is a good variable name to store the count of the number of times pin 12 has changed from high to low?

On-time, off-time, period and duty cycle

With our new skill at using variables, we can re-write the blink sketch with variables and make it a general pulse train synthesizer.

We will create a repeating pattern of on-times and off-times. We can describe this pattern in one of two ways:

- *in terms of an independent on-time and an off-time*
- *in terms of a repeat period and a fraction of the time it is on, which we call the duty cycle*

I like using the period and duty cycle to control the LED. This is a more intuitive set of figures of merit. To modulate the LED, and use the principles of the BLINK code, we will need to translate the *period* and *duty cycle* into the on and off times.

This is very simple. The on-time and off-time are:

onTime_sec = Period_sec x dutyCycle

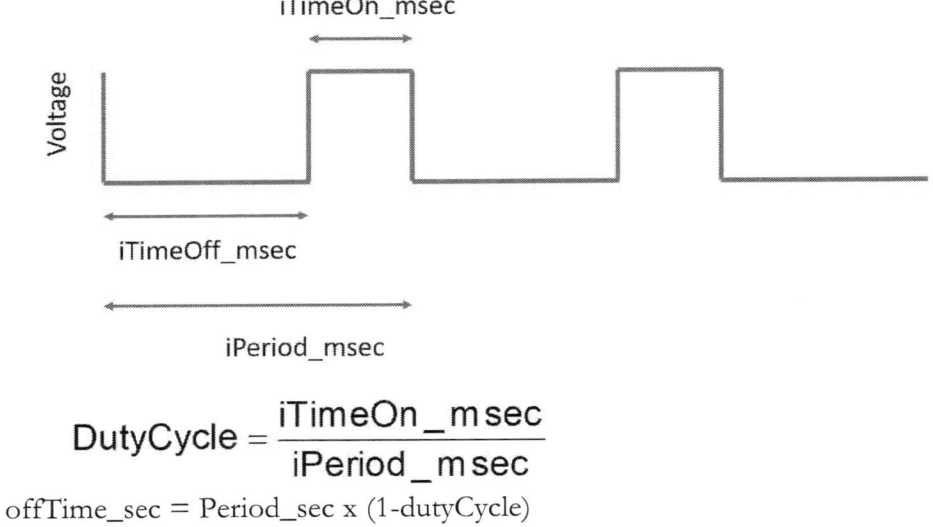

$$\text{DutyCycle} = \frac{\text{iTimeOn\_msec}}{\text{iPeriod\_msec}}$$

offTime_sec = Period_sec x (1-dutyCycle)

The pattern of on and off times of the LED when it is modulated.

The duty cycle controls the apparent brightness of the LED. A duty cycle of 90% means the LED is on for most of the period and it will look bright to us. A duty cycle of only 10% means the LED is on for only a small fraction of the period and it will look dim to our eye.

We will modulate the LED with a period that is short enough so that our eye can't tell the LED is pulsing off and on.

To make the LED flash fast enough so we can't see it flashing, we want the period to be shorter than about 40 msec, or the flash frequency to be faster than 1/40 msec = 25 Hz.

This means we can adjust the on-time from 0 msec to 40 msec. We use delay() commands to adjust the on and off times.

A modified BLINK is all we need to drive the LED with a pulse train. We'll start with a period of 0.040 seconds (40 msec) and adjust the duty cycle from 0% to 100%.

Try this experiment: How would you write the code to set the period and duty cycle for the LED using variables? Use a period of 1 second and adjust the duty cycle. This way you can see the fraction of the time the LED is on.

Make the period shorter and shorter until it is shorter than the flicker rate and watch the LED transition from flashing to appearing on continuously.

> If you get stuck, watch this video and I will walk you through setting up this experiment.

87

My sketch to modulate the LED with a period and duty cycle

```
// introducing variables

long iPeriod_msec = 500;

float dutyCycle_fraction = 0.5;

long iTimeOn_msec = iPeriod_msec * dutyCycle_fraction;

long iTimeOff_msec = iPeriod_msec - iTimeOn_msec;

void setup() {
    PINMODE(13, OUTPUT);
}

void loop() {
    DIGITALWRITE(13, HIGH);
    DELAY(iTimeOn_msec);
    DIGITALWRITE(13, LOW);
    DELAY(iTimeOff_msec);
}
```

Summary of the commands introduced so far

Command	Description
void setup (){ }	This is a function that appears in EVERY sketch. Every command within the brackets will be executed just once
void loop (){ }	This is a function that appears in EVERY sketch. Every command within the brackets will execute over and over again.
PINMODE(13, OUTPUT);	This command tells the Arduino that we are going to use

	a specific digital pin as an OUTPUT, as distinct from an INPUT. We use the pin number to identify the pin we want to setup.
DIGITALWRITE(13, HIGH);	This command controls the output of a digital pin and makes it either a HIGH (logic 1, or 5 V) or a LOW (a logic 0 or a 0 V). Once executed, the pin value will be set to this value.
DELAY(1000);	This command tells the Arduino to sit there, twiddling

	its thumbs, doing nothing for a duration of milliseconds as listed inside the (). In this example, the time interval to wait is 1000 msec = 1 sec.
`//` or `/*` `*/`	Comments. Everything after these two forward slashes will be ignored by the Arduino sketch. We can use this add comments for our own benefit on any line. For multiple lines add them between the /*

		and the */ lines.
Serial.begin(9600);		This command opens up the serial com link with a baud rated inside the (). In this example the baud rate is 9600 baud. The name Serial is an object, the serial link. The .BEGIN is a verb, telling the object to get set up.
Serial.PRINT("Hello World");		This command will print characters to the serial communications channel. Everything inside the () will

	be printed. To print a string, enclose the characters within quotes. After printing, the cursor will be left on the same line.
Serial.PRINTLN(" ");	Does the same thing as the Serial.PRINT command, but moves the cursor to the next line after printing the characters. This starts the next printed content on a new line.
Serial monitor	The terminal emulator that you can print to. This is the

	primary way of displaying information from the Arduino.
int, long	This will create a new variable that will store an integer. This is a whole number. It is usually placed before the setup() function
float	This will create a new variable that will store a floating point number. This is a number that has a decimal point. It is usually placed before the

| | setup() function |

Chapter 4 Coding for the Arduino

Coding a program for Arduino means learning a new language, but it is not as hard as you might think. In the same way that mathematics has its own set of symbols to denote various functions like addition, subtraction, and multiplication, there are different symbols and terms used when coding for Arduino. If you have had experience working with coding in the past, learning a new language is easy. For those of you who have never learned to code, translating one form of code to another is like translating one language to another. Though this may seem difficult, the idea of coding is to make coding for other programs easier in the future. Below is a list of the terms and words that are used in Arduino IDE coding and how to use them.

Structure

setup()

This is the function called on when the sketch starts and will run only once after startup or reset. You can use it to start variables, pin modes, or the use of libraries (specific terms you can download for extra functionality).

loop()

The loop function requires the Arduino microcontroller board to repeat a function multiple times, continuously or until a certain variable or condition is met. You will set the condition for it to stop the loop or you will have it loop continuously until you detach the Arduino from the power source or turn it off.

CONTROL STRUCTURES

Control structures show how an input will be received. Just like the name implies, various inputs regarding control determine how your data will be read. Provisional language will also be considered in data analysis. Popular and various control structures are mentioned below.

If

This is what links a condition or input to an output. It means that *if* a certain condition has been met, a specific output or response of the microcontroller will occur. For example, *if* the thermometer to which the microcontroller is attached measures more than 75 degrees Fahrenheit, you might write the code to direct the Arduino to send a signal to your air conditioning unit to turn on to decrease the temperature back to 75 degrees.

If...Else

This is like the *If* conditional, but it specifies another action that the microcontroller will take if the condition for the first action is not met. This gives you an option of performing two different actions in two different circumstances with one piece of code.

While

This is a loop that will continue indefinitely until the expression to which it is connected becomes false. That is, it would perform a certain function until a parameter is met and the statement that is set as the condition is made false.

Do… While

This is like the *while* statement, but it always runs at least once because it tests the variable at the end of the function rather than at the beginning.

Break

This is an emergency exit of sorts from a function of the microcontroller. It is used to exit a *do, for,* or *while* loop without meeting the condition that must be met to exit that part of the functionality.

Continue

Return

This is the way to stop a function, and it returns a value with which the function terminated to the calling function or the function that is asking for the information.

Goto

This piece of code tells the microcontroller to move to another place, not consecutive, in the coded program. It transfers the flow to another place in the program. Its use is generally discouraged by C language programmers, but it can definitely simplify a program.

SYNTAX

; (semicolon)

This is used as a period in the English language: it ends a statement. Be sure, however, that the statement closed by the semicolon is complete, or else your code will not function properly.

{} (curly braces)

These have many complex functions, but the thing you must know is that when you insert a beginning curly brace, you *must* follow it with an ending curly brace. This is called keeping the braces balanced and is vital to getting your program working.

// (single-line comment)

If you would like to remind yourself or tell others something about how your code functions, use this code to begin the comment and make sure that it only takes up one line. This will not transfer to the processor of the microcontroller but rather will live in the code and be a reference to you and anyone who is reading the code manually.

/* */ (multi-line comment)

This type of comment is opened by the /*, and it spans more than one line. It can itself contain a single line comment but cannot contain another multi-line comment. Be sure to close the comment with */ or else the rest of your code will be considered a comment and not implemented.

#define

This defines a certain variable as a constant value. It gives a name to that value as a sort of shorthand for that value. These do not take up any memory space on the chip so they can be useful in conserving space. Once the code is compiled or taken together as a program, the compiler will replace any instance of the constant as the value that is used to define it.

NOTE: This statement does NOT use a semicolon at the end.

#include

This is used to include other libraries in your sketch, that is, to include other words and coding language in your sketch that would not otherwise be included. For example, you could include AVR C libraries or many tools, or pieces of code, from the various C libraries.

NOTE: Do NOT add the semicolon at the end of this statement, just as you would exclude it from the *#define* statement. If you do include a semicolon to close the statement, you will receive error messages and the program will not work.

ARITHMETIC OPERATORS

Just as the name implies, arithmetic operators complete codes through use of mathematical symbols. Each symbol connects one line of code to another. When looking for an output resulting in measured values, be sure to check your Arduino setup. Connecting wire with Arduino in the wrong voltage receptors may lead to negative or irrelevant values.

= (assignment operator)

This assigns a value to a variable and replaces the variable with the assigned value throughout the operation in which it appears. This is different than == which evaluates whether two variables or a variable and a set value are equal. The double equal signs function more like the single equal sign in mathematics and algebra than the single equal sign in the Arduino IDE.

+ (addition)

This does what you might expect it would do: it adds two values, or the value to a variable, or two to a fixed constant. One thing that you must take into account is that there is a maximum for variable values in the C programming languages. This means that, if your variable maxes out at 32,767, then adding 1 to the variable will give you a negative result, -32,768. If you expect that the values will be greater than the absolute maximum value allowable, you can still perform the operations, but you will have to instruct the microcontroller what to do in the case of negative results. In addition, as well as in subtraction, multiplication, and division, you place the resulting variable on the left and the operation to the right of the = or ==.

Also, another thing to keep in mind is that whatever type of data you input into the operation will determine the type of data that is output by the operation. We will look at types of data later, but for example, if you input integers, which are whole numbers, you will receive an answer rounded to the nearest whole number.

- (subtraction)

This operation, like the addition sign, does what you would expect: it subtracts two values from each other, whether they both are variables, or one is a constant value. Again, you will have to watch out for values greater than the maximum integer value. Remember to place the resulting variable on the left of the equal sign or signs, and the operation on the right.

* (multiplication)

With multiplication especially, you will need to be careful to define what happens if the value you receive from the operation is greater than the greatest allowable value of a piece of data. This is because multiplication especially grows numbers to large, large values.

/ (division)

Remember to place the resulting variable on the left of the operation, and the values that you are dividing on the right side of the operation.

% (modulo)

This operation gives you the remainder when an integer is divided by another integer. For example, if you did $y = 7 \% 5$, the result for y would be 2, since five goes into seven once and leaves a remainder of 2. Remember, you must use integer values for this type of operation.

COMPARISON OPERATORS

Comparison operators compare the values from the left side of the equation to the right. If the left operator does not have the same units as the right, it is still possible to use these operators, but the results may be unpredictable (Arduino.cc).

== (equal to)

This operator checks to see if the data on the left side of the double equal signs match the data on the right side, that is, whether they are equal. For example, you might ask the pin attached to the temperature gauge *t* == *75*, and if the temperature is exactly 75 degrees, then the microcontroller will perform a certain task, whether it be turning off the heating or cooling, or turning off a fan.

!= (not equal to)

This is the mirror image of the previous operation. You could just as easily write a program to test *t* != *75* and set up the microcontroller to turn on a heating lamp, turn on a fan, or ignite the wood in the fireplace if this statement is true. Between == and !=, you can cover all the possible conditions that input might give your microcontroller.

< (less than)

If this statement is true, then you can program a certain response from your microcontroller, or, in other words, program output for such input.

> (greater than)

INPUT

In the input state, a digital pin will require very little of the processing power and energy from the microcontroller and battery. Instead, it is simply measuring and indicating to the microcontroller its measurements.

OUTPUT

These are very good at powering LED's because they are in a low-impedance state, meaning they let the energy flow freely through them without much resistance. Output pins take their directions from the microcontroller once it has processed the information given by the input pins, and the output pins power whatever mechanism will perform the intended task.

INPUT_PULLUP

This is what mode you will want to use when connected to a button or a switch. There is a lot of resistance involved in the INPUT_PULLUP state. This means that it is best used for Boolean-like situations, such as a switch either being on or off. When there are only two states and not much in between, use INPUT_PULLUP.

LED_BUILTTIN

true

In a Boolean sense, any integer that is not zero is true. One is true, 200 is true, -3 is true, etc. This would be the case when a statement matches reality. One of your pins might be testing a value, and the statement is trying to match $y \mathrel{!=} 35$, so if the pin receives information that the value of y is 25, then the statement $25 \mathrel{!=} 35$ is true.

false

This is part of a Boolean Constant, meaning that a statement is false, or that its logic does not match reality. For example, you could have a statement, $x > 7$ and the value the microcontroller receives for x is 3. This would make the statement *false*. It would then be defined as 0 (zero).

integer constants

These are constants that are used by the sketch directly and are in base 10 form, or integer form. You can change the form that the integer constants are written in by preceding the integer with a special notation signifying binary notation (base 2), the octal notation (base 8), or hexadecimal notation (base 16), for example.

floating point constants

These save space in the program by creating a shorthand for a long number in scientific notation. Each time the floating-point constant appears, it is evaluated at the value that you dictate in your code.

DATA TYPES

Data types refer to the type of data received in each of the programming setups you apply. Data received by Arduino are sent to your program of choice to determine various outcomes. Some examples are listed below.

Void

This is used in a function declaration to tell the microcontroller that no information is expected to be returned with this function. For example, you would use it with the *setup()* or *loop()* functions.

Boolean

Boolean data holds one of two values: true or false. This could be true of any of the arithmetic operator functions or of other functions. You will use *&&* if you want two conditions to be true simultaneously for the Boolean to be true, || if you want one of two conditions to be met, either one setting off the output response, and ! for not true, meaning that if the operator is *not* true, then the Boolean is true.

Char

This is a character, such as a letter. It also has a numeric value, such that you can perform arithmetic functions on letters and characters. If you want to use characters literally, you will use a single quote for a single character, '*A*' and a double quote for multiple characters, "*ABC*" such that all characters are enclosed in quotes. This means the microcontroller will output these characters verbatim if the given conditions are met. The numbers -128 to 127 are used to signify various signed characters.

Unsigned Char

This is the same as a character but uses the numbers 0 to 255 to signify characters instead of the "signed" characters which include negatives. This is the same as the byte datatype.

Byte

This type of data stores a number from 0 to 255 in an 8-bit system of binary numbers. For example, B10010 is the number 18, because this uses a base 2 system.

Int

Integers are how you will store numbers for the most part. Because most Arduinos have a 16-bit system, the minimum value is -32,768 and the maximum value of an integer is 32,767. The Arduino Due and a few other boards work on a 32-bit system, and thus can carry integers ranging from -2,147,483,648 to 2,147,483,647. Remember these numbers when you are attempting arithmetic with your program, as any numbers higher or lower than these values will cause errors in your code.

Unsigned Int

This yields the ability to store numbers from 0 to 65,535 on the 8-bit boards with which you will likely be working. If you have higher values than the signed integers will allow, you can switch to unsigned integers and achieve the same amount of range but all in the positive realm, such that you have a higher absolute value of the range.

Word

A word stores a 16-bit unsigned number on the Uno and on other boards with which you will likely be working. In using the Due and the Zero, you will be storing 32-bit numbers using words. Word is essentially the means by which integers and numbers are stored.

Long

If you need to store longer numbers, you can access 4-byte storage, or 32-bit storage in other words, using the long variable. You simply follow an integer in your coded math with the capital letter L. This will achieve numbers from -2,147,483,648 to 2,147,483,647.

Unsigned Long

The way to achieve the largest numbers possible and store the largest integers possible is to direct the microcontroller using the unsigned long variables. This also gives you 32 bits or 4 bytes to work with, but being unassigned the 32nd bit is freed from indicating the positive or negative sign in order to give you access to numbers from 0 to 4,294,967,295.

Short

This is simply another way of indicating a 16-bit datatype. On every type of Arduino, you can use short to indicate you are expecting or using integers from -32,768 to 32,767. This helps free up space on your Due or Zero by not wasting space on 0's for a small number and by halving the number of bits used to store that number.

Float

A float number is a single digit followed by 6 to 7 decimal places, multiplied by 10 to a power up to 38. This can be used to store more precise numbers or just larger numbers. Float numbers take a lot more processing power to calculate and work with, and they only have 6 to 7 decimals of precision, so they are not useful in all cases. Many programmers actually try to convert as much float math to integer math as possible to speed up the processing. In addition, these take 32 bits to store versus the normal 16 bits, so if you're running low on storage, try converting your float numbers to integers.

Double

This is only truly relevant to the Due, in which doubling allows for double the precision of a float number. For all other Arduino boards, the floating-point number always takes up 32 bits, so floating does nothing to increase precision or accuracy.

Chapter 5 Ultrasonic Sensor

This sensor is going to be able to determine how far an object is by using a system that is similar to the system that bats use. It is going to give you a great no contact range detection that is highly accurate and going to produce stable readings.

This operation is not going to be affected by things like sunlight or black material, but soft materials such as cloth are going to b somewhat difficult for the sensor to pick up. It is going to be complete with an ultrasonic transmitter and receiver module.

Tech Specifications

1. Measuring angle: thirty degrees
2. Power supply: five volts
3. Resolution: point three cm
4. *Quiescent current: greater than two milliamps.*
5. Ranging distance: two to four hundred cm
6. Working current: fifteen milliamps

Effectual angel: greater than fifteen degrees

Components

1. Arduino Uno R3 (1)
2. Breadpanel (1)

Ultrasonic sensor (1)

Code

Const int ping pin = 7 ; // trigger pin with sensor

```
Const in echo pin = 6 ; /// echo the pin with the sensor

Void setup () {

Serial begin (9600) ; // start serial terminal

}

Void loop () {

Long duration, inches, cm ;

Pin mode (ping pin, output) ;

Digital write (ping pin, low) ;

Delay microseconds (3) ;

Digital write (ping pin, high( ;

Delay microseconds (4) ;

Digital write (ping pin, low) ;

Pin mode (echo pin, input) ;

Duration = pulse in (echo pin, high ) ;

Inches = microseconds to inches (duration) ;

Cm = microseconds to centimeters (duration) ;

Serial print (inches) ;

Serial print ( in, ) ;

Serial print (cm) ;
```

Serial print (cm) ;

Serial print in () ;

Delay (499) ;

}

Long microseconds to inches (long microseconds) {

Return microseconds / 49 / 2 ;

}

Long microseconds to centimeters (long microseconds) {

Return microseconds / 49 / 2 ;

}

Code notes
1. Connect the GND to the GND
2. The positive five-volt pin to the positive five volt
3. The echo to pin six

The trigger to pin seven

Result

You are going to see the distance measured by your sensor in inches and centimeters.

CONCLUSION

Congratulations! Now you have everything you need to go out on your own and start building the projects of your dreams. You learned how to connect any kind of module in order to extend the functionality of the Arduino board, and now you can finally start building more complex projects, such as robots! Start taking over the world and share everything with other Arduino fans and extend your knowledge about electronics, computers, and programming.

Remember, if you feel intimidated by certain topics, or if you think you aren't that great at coding, you shouldn't give up! There's a solution for everything and there are many online communities out there willing to help. Explore the applications step by step, read more module datasheets and reference guides, examine project schematics, and start building. The things you can achieve with the Arduino are incredible, and you should continue practicing because nobody becomes an engineer or a developer overnight without practice.

Congratulations on continuing with the Arduino guide series and advancing to the next level! Keep this guide close, and continue expanding your knowledge with more books, more tutorials, and more practice. Start building your army of Arduino robots today and conquer the world, because why not?

ARDUINO PROGRAMMING

THE PRACTICAL **INTERMEDIATE'S** GUIDE TO LEARN ARDUINO PROGRAMMING IN ONE DAY STEP-BY-STEP
(#2020 UPDATED VERSION | EFFECTIVE COMPUTER LANGUAGES)

STEVE TUDOR

Text Copyright ©

All rights reserved. No part of this guide may be reproduced in any form without permission in writing from the publisher except in the case of brief quotations embodied in critical articles or reviews.

Legal & Disclaimer

The information contained in this book and its contents is not designed to replace or take the place of any form of medical or professional advice; and is not meant to replace the need for independent medical, financial, legal or other professional advice or services, as may be required. The content and information in this book has been provided for educational and entertainment purposes only.

The content and information contained in this book has been compiled from sources deemed reliable, and it is accurate to the best of the Author's knowledge, information and belief. However, the Author cannot guarantee its accuracy and validity and cannot be held liable for any errors and/or omissions. Further, changes are periodically made to this book as and when needed. Where appropriate and/or necessary, you must consult a professional (including but not limited to your doctor, attorney, financial advisor or such other professional advisor) before using any of the suggested remedies, techniques, or information in this book.

Upon using the contents and information contained in this book, you agree to hold harmless the Author from and against any damages, costs, and expenses, including any legal fees potentially resulting from the application of any of the information provided by this book. This disclaimer applies to any loss, damages or injury caused by the use and application, whether directly or indirectly, of any advice or information presented, whether for breach of contract, tort, negligence, personal injury, criminal intent, or under any other cause of action.

You agree to accept all risks of using the information presented inside this book.

You agree that by continuing to read this book, where appropriate and/or necessary, you shall consult a professional (including but not limited to your doctor, attorney, or financial advisor or such other advisor as needed) before using any of the suggested remedies, techniques, or information in this book.

Introduction

In case you've never heard of an Arduino before, it is an open-source electronic interface that has two parts: the first is the programable circuit board, and the other is a coding program of your choice to run to your computer. Arduinos come in many forms, including the Arduino Uno, LilyPad Arduino, Redboard, Arduino Mega, Arduino Leonardo, and others which we will explain later on.

If you're unfamiliar with programming, this is a good place to start. The Arduino can be programmed in various types of programming languages, and its wide array of Arduino options can give you more programming experience. Arduinos come with additional attachments, some in the form of sensors, and others can be obtained anywhere and can be attached to the various ports on an Arduino. Arduino is a great stepping stone on the way to understanding programming and sensor interaction.

In programming languages, there is always the well-known program, "Hello World" that is showcased on the screen. In the microcontroller world that we are in, this phase or first program is indicated by a blinking of the light, "on" and "off" to show that everything you have set up works correctly.

We will look at the sketches in their entirety and explain the details after explaining the code. If you go through something that you cannot make something out of, keep on reading, and it will be clear.

Let us look at this program, to show you how we will be breaking down the codes.

Const int PinkL = 13;

Void setup ()

{ pinMode (PinkL, OUTPUT); }

Void loop ()

{digitalWrite(PinkL, HIGH);

delay (600);

digitalWrite(PinkL, LOW);

delay(600); }

On the first part

Const int PinkL = 13;

This line is used to define a constant that is used throughout the program to specify a particular value. All pins are recommended to have this because it makes it easy for software change if the circuit is still the same. In programming in Arduino, the constants are commonly named starting with the letter "k".

The second tc part

Void setup ()

{pinMode (PinkL, OUTPUT);}

The OUTPUT is pin 13. This now makes Arduino control the coding to the pins, instead of reading from it.

The third part

Void loop()

{digitalWrite (PinkL, HIGH);

delay(600);

digitalWrite(PinkL, LOW);

Delay(600);}

This is where the core part of the code is. A HIGH is written to the pin that leads to the turning of the LED. When you place HIGH, it means that 5V is the pin's output. The other option we have is LOW, which means that you are putting 0V out.

A delay() is called to delay the number of milliseconds that is sent to it. Since we send 600, there will be a delay of 0.6 of a second. The LED goes off, and this is attributed to the LOW that is written as an output on the pin.

A 600 milliseconds delay will be activated.

This will be the sequence until the Arduino goes off or the power is disconnected from it.

Before you start digesting more content, try this program out and ensure that it works just fine. To test if you have set your LED in reverse order, the following might happen. On the UNO board, you have pin 13 connected to a Light Emitting Diode connected. When it blinks and the breadboard LED does not blink, then you might have connected your

LED in reverse. In case you see that it is blinking once in a second, then the program has not been sent to the Arduino successfully.

When you've completed the programming, place comments in the coding lines to instruct the Arduino. These comments can instruct your Arduino to blink the LED intermittently or through various sequences.

The programs we normally write are usually meant for the computers and not for people to understand once they are opened up. There is a good provision that allows us, humans, to read the program easily and the computer will have no clue about it. There are two comments that are possible in this program:

1. The block comment style starts with two characters, /* which progresses until */ is seen. Multiple lines are then crossed and here are a few examples.

/* This is the first line*/

/* the program was successful*/

/* we

*are

*going

*far */

2. Commenting can be done on a line that has the backslash operator //. This is the part that is meant for humans and not machines. It is another way to insert a comment.

When you add comments in a program, you will have a code that looks like the statement above.

You will find in the following pages, that if there is no number next to the line of code, it indicates a comment continuation from the line at the top. We might not showcase this in perfection because we are using a limited space in our book. You will find a hyphen at the line's end that is continued and a hyphen along the continuation line. This is just our way of handling it, but in an IDE, you won't find it and you need not type them.

/*

* Program Name: Blink123

*Author: James Aden

* Date written: 24 July 2017

*Description:

* Turns an LED on for a sixth-hundred of a second, then for another sixth-hundred of a- -second on a continuous repetitive session

*/

/* Pin Definitions */

Const int PinkL = 13;

/*

*Functions Name: setup

*Purpose: Run once after system power up

*/

Void setup() {pinMode(PinkL,OUTPUT);}

/*

Void loop() {digitalWrite(PinkL,HIGH);Delay(600);digitalWrite(PinkL,LOW); Delay(600):}

Gotchas

If you find out that your program does not compile, or it gives you a different result than what you need, here are a few things that people get confused about:

The programming language is normally sensitive to capitalization of letters. For instance, myVar is considered different to MyVar.

Tabs, blank lines, and white spaces are equivalent to a single space, making it easier for one to read.

Code blocks are normally grouped using curly braces, i.e., "{" and "}"

All open parenthesis have a corresponding closing parenthesis, i.e. "(" and ")"

Numbers don't have commas. So instead of writing 1,000, ensure that you write 1000.

All program statements MUST end with a semicolon. This means that each statement except for the following two cases:

-In comments

- after curly braces are placed "}"

Assignment task to test what you have learned:

1. Alter the delay time of your LED before it comes back on to stick to 1.5 seconds. Leave the ON time of the LED limited to 600 milliseconds.

2. From pin 13, change to pin 2, making it the new connection to the LED. Keep in mind that both the circuit & and the program will be different.

This is just a basis for basic Arduino programming. In the rest of the book, we will be looking at how Arduinos can be programmed with respect to different functions. If you're new to programming, don't let the above codes frighten you. Coding takes practice, but it relatively easy to learn, just like a new language.

Chapter 1   Key   Terms   in   Understanding Arduino

hen working with Arduino technologies, it is helpful to understand the terminology of Arduino. You will need to understand the terminology to choose a board, write the coded instructions, set up the microcontroller for use, and finally using the Arduino board. In this chapter, you will find some key terms that will aid you greatly in your endeavor to become an Arduino user.

As mentioned earlier, Arduino is open-source, meaning you can use it and teach it to others without violating any copyright laws. It is based on easy-to-use hardware, which is the actual physical computer board with which you will be working, and straightforward software, the coded instructions with which you will use to direct the hardware to perform a task of your choosing. The software is also known as code, and the individual pieces of instructions are called tools.

Anatomy of the Arduino Board

The board itself contains a good number of parts. The digital pins run along the edges of most Arduino microcontrollers and are used for input, or sensing of a condition, and output, the response that the controller makes to the input. For example, the input might be that the light sensor senses darkness, that is, a lack of light. It will then close a circuit lighting up a bulb as output: a nightlight for your child.

On most boards, there will be a Pin LED, associated with a specific pin, like Pin 13 on the Arduino Uno. This Pin LED is the only output possibility built into the board, and it will help you with your first project of a "blink sketch," which will be explained later. The Pin LED is also used for debugging or fixing the code you have written so that it has no mistakes in it. The Power LED is what its name implies: it lights up when the board is receiving power or is "turned on." This can also be helpful in debugging your code.

There exists on every board the microcontroller itself, called the ATmega microcontroller, which is the brain of the entire board. It receives your instructions and acts accordingly. Without this, the entire board would have no functionality.

Analog in pins exist on the opposite edge of the board from the digital pins on the Arduino Uno. It is an input into the Arduino system. Analog means that the signal which is input is not constant but instead varies with time, such as audio input. In the example of audio input, the auditory input in a room varies with the people in the room talking and with the noises filtering in from outside the room.

GND and 5V pins are used to create additional power of 5V to the circuit and microcontroller. The power connector is most often on the edge of the Arduino board, and it is used to provide power to the microcontroller when it is not plugged into the USB. The USB port can be used as a power source as well, but its main function is to upload, or transfer, your sketch, or set of instructions that you have coded, from your computer to the Arduino.

TX and RX LED's are used to indicate that there is a transfer of information occurring. This indication of communication will happen when you upload your sketches from your computer to the Arduino so that they will blink rapidly during the exchange.

The reset button is as it sounds: it resets the microcontroller to factory settings and erases any information you have uploaded to the Arduino.

Other Terms about Working with Arduino

There are three types of memory in an Arduino system. Memory is the space where information is stored.

Flash memory is where the code for the program that you have written is stored. It is also called the "program space," because it is used for the program automatically when you upload it to the Arduino. This type of memory remains intact when the power is cut off, or when the Arduino is turned off.

SRAM (static random-access memory) is the space used by the sketch or program you have created to create, store, and work with information from the input sources to create an output. This type of storage disappears once the power is turned off.

EEPROM is like a tiny a hard-drive that allows the programmer to store information other than the program itself when the Arduino is turned off. There are separate instructions for the EEPROM, for reading, writing, and erasing, as well as other functions.

Certain digital pins will be designated as PWM pins, meaning that they can create analog using digital means. Analog, as we remember, means that input (or output) is varied and not constant. Normally, digital pins can only create a constant flow of energy. However, PWM pins can vary the "pulse" of energy between 0 and 5 Volts. Certain tasks that you program can only be carried out by PWM pins.

In addition, in comparing microcontroller boards, you will want to look at clock speed, which is the speed at which the microcontroller operates. The faster the speed, the more responsive it the board will be, but the more battery or energy it will consume as well.

UART measures the number of serial communication lines the device can handle. Serial communication lines are lines that transfer data serially, that is, in a line rather than in parallel or simultaneously. It requires much less hardware to process things serially than in parallel.

Some projects will have you connecting devices to the Internet of Things, which essentially describes the interconnectedness of devices, other than desktop and laptop computers, to various networks in order to share information. Everything from smart refrigerators, to smartphones, to smart TV's are connected to the Internet of Things.

Chapter 2 Working with User-Defined Functions

Another thing that we need to take a look at before we end this guidebook is the idea of the user defined function. One of the methods that you are able to keep the code that you are writing, in Arduino and in other languages, clean and organized and modular or reusable, is to make sure that you work with functions inside of that code. In addition, these functions are able to make some of the code smaller because parts of the code, and small sections of it, can be reusable. Functions are going to be like tools that were created in order to serve the particular function that you would like, just like the name is going to suggest.

While we have already gone through and encountered some examples of these particular functions as we go through this guidebook, we now need to go through some of the details that come with them and really understand some of the parts that go with them. This is going to help us to explain some of the features that we may have glossed over in the first place, so that we really know what these functions are like.

The first thing that we are able to do here is to look at the declaration of the function that we want to work with. A good example of how to do this is going to be below:

float employeeEarnings (float hoursWorked, float payrate) {

float results: // this will be the value that we are going to return when this function has been called up. We want to make sure that it is going to match the type of data that we are using before the name of the function

results = hoursWorked * payrate

Return results // return tells the function that it needs to send a value back once to where it was originally called.

}

Take some time to look over that code and see what it is able to offer in terms of what you are able to do with it, and even what you are able to understand out of the code based on what we have already been able to work with. You can even get some practice in order to get better at this by typing the code out a few times and gaining a feel for it.

This function is going to take on two arguments in order to be successful. It is going to be with the hoursWorked and the payRate in order to handle some of the work that we are doing, and both of these are going to be floats. It does take us some time to work on simple math on these and then it is going to return a float as the value.

The return that we are working on here means that we want to end or terminate the function and then send back the value that was placed with us, after the word return, which is usually going to be a variable, as the results of the calculations that we did. All of this is going to be done to help us understand how these functions work and how we are able to do some stuff with them.

With this in mind, we then need to go through and call up this function. This will allow us to see what the earnings of the employee's are, and can make it easier to see what we are going to get out of this process as well when we work with some of the functions. The code that we are going to need to work with to make this happen will include:

void loop () {

floathoursWorked = 37.5;

float payRate = 18.50;

float result = employeeEarnings (hoursWorked, payRate)

// results will be 693.75

This is a pretty straightforward cod that we are able to work with, but it is definitely going to show us what we are able to do here, and why all of the parts are going to be important along the way. it is also a simple way to get some ideas on how the function is going to work overall.

The first thing that we are going to find here is that the function we want to declare has to be declared independent of and outside of the other functions. This means that we need to be able to write the code for the function that we want to create, doing so either inside of the loop function or the setup function. You can also work with some of the other user defined functions that are there.

We can also go with this and look at another example that will make it easier to see how this is supposed to work. We are going to look at a sample sketch here that is going to be used in many cases to help us smooth out some of our readings of the sensors:

```
int sensorSmoothin (analogPin) {

in sensorValue = 0;

for (int index = 0; index < 5, index ++)

digitalWrite(LED_BUILTIN, HIGH); //Turn on the LED for smoothing.

sensorValue= sensorValue + analogRead (analogPin)

delay(100) // 100 millisecond delay between the samples

}

digitalWrite(LED_BUILTIN, LOW); //turn off the LED

sensorValue = sensorValue / 5 //average the values over five samples that we are using.

return sensorValue;

}
```

As you go through some of this, you are going to find that this is going to show up a lot of the functions that we were talking about earlier on. This is going to make it so much easier for us to feel comfortable with some of the work that we are trying to do along the way. The more time that you spend working on some of the coding that we want to do along the way, the easier it is to work with the code because we are comfortable and can recognize things along the way.

This is a good function to work with because it is going to be used to help us to smooth out the input of the data of many sensors, especially if you find that they are prone to inputs that are a bit jittery in the process. This is going to work well because it is able to average out the sample to give us a more consistent flow of data. We are able to see that the code we just did above is going to be similar to some of the sample that we did in the beginning. Let's take along look at it to see what it did there:

With all of this, we are going to be able to work on initializing our sensorValue variable so that it is going to be able to call up the sensorSmoothing() function that we need. This is all going to happen on the analog pin of 0, and can help us out here because it is going to make sure that we are able to average out the results that we have over not just one sample, but over five samples that we are able to use.

Of course, we have to remember that the functions we are working with are not going to always be as smooth and easy to work with as this example. The functions are not always going to need to have parameters or return variables in order to work either. Sometimes the functions can be set up to return no value, and then they can also have no parameters in the process either. All that they are going to do when you bring them up is to execute the few lines of code that you want, and then you can terminate it all, bringing the compiler back to the place in the code where you called them from.

As you can see, these user defined functions are not going to be as difficult as they may seem in the beginning. With a bit of practice, and even trying out a few of the functions that we were able to work with in this chapter, and doing some of your own, you will find that you are able to make these user defined functions work the way that you would like and they will help your Arduino technology complete the project.

Chapter 3 The Serial

While you are not necessarily able to implement the stream class in itself, you are able to go through and implement some of the derivatives of it, and this is where we are going to find a lot of the utility that we need. The serial class that we are going with here is going to be an extension of what we are able to do with the stream class, and it is going to help us to communicate with some of the other devices that we want, such as the computer.

The serial is going to be enacted through both the port on the Arduino for the Serial, as well as on the link for the USB on the computer. We are going to then look at some of the functions that are available with the Serial class, making it easier for you to use this kind of thing and get the most out of this resource along the way as well:

1. Serial.begin(rate): you are already familiar with how this one is going to work. It is a good one to use to help us start out the serial transmission of our data. You are also able to specify the specific rate of the data transmission that you are getting and see it in bits per second.
2. Serial.end): This function is going to allow us to end the communication through this. You can then go through and restart the communication by working with the Serial.begin() function that we did before. While the communication is disabled for whatever purpose, you are able to use the serial pins for generalized entry and exit of the data.

3. Serial.find(string): This is the one that is going to search for the given string within the data that is provided by the Serial. If the string is found, then the method is going to return true. If the string is not found, then the method is going to return the output of false to us.
4. Serial.findUntil(string, OPTIONAL endString): This one is going to take some time to look for a specific string within a serial buffer, until either the string is found or the specified terminating string is found. If the target string is found, then the method is going to return true to us. If the terminating string is found or if the method times out, then you are going to get a return of false.
5. Serial.flush(): This one is going to all you time to halt a process until all of the data that is being sent to the serial has been sent.
6. Serial.parseFloat(): This function is going to work for us by returning the first floating point number to be provided with the serial stream. It is often going to be brought to an end with any character that is not seen as a floating point.
7. Serial.parseInt(): This one is going to be able to work by returning the first integer number to be provided by the serial stream. It is going to be brought to an end by the first character that you are working with that isn't a digit.
8. Serial.peek(): This one is going to return the very next character that should be imported by the serial buffer. However it is not going to remove any of the character from

the bugger. This makes it a bit different than he Serial.read() method that we will talk about soon. This means that you are just going to be able to see which of the characters are coming next.

9. Serial.pint(value, OPTIONAL format): You are able to specify the format as well as an option. Otherwise, the integers are going to print as decimals by default. The foats are going to print with two decimal places by default, and so on. You are able to send strings or characters as is to the print statement, and it is going to do the printing that you need without any issues.

10. Serial.pintln(value, OPTIONAL format): This one is going to allow you to prin out some of the values, just like we would expect with some of the other print methods out there.

11. Serial.read(): This one is going to be able to read the data that is showing up through your serial port. This is going to be added to some of the incoming stream of serial data and it is known as the serial buffer. When you read from this buffer, the information will then be destroyed, so we need to make sure that we are saving the data to a variable if we wish to reuse it at one point or another.

12. Serial.readBytes: This one is going to help us read in the characters from the serial port to the buffer. You are able to determine the number of bytes that you would like to see read. Your buffer has to be an array that is a byte or a char.

13. Serial.readBytesUntil: This one is going to work on reading the characters from the serial port, either until the given

number of bytes has been read through on there, or until the chosen terminating character is read through as well. In either case, the method will then be able to terminate.

14. Serial.write(): This one is going to write out the data to the serial port. But this method is only going to send over data that is binary to the serial port. If you need to send over other kinds of data, like ASCII, you will need to work with the print method instead.

15. Serial.serialEvent(): The last method that we are going to take some time looking at is this one. Whenever the data you need comes to be available for use with your port of he serial, then this is going to be the function that is called. You can then use this function to help us read the data from the serial port.

As we can see here, we have spent a good deal of time talking about a lot of different topics, especially the functions that we are able to use when we are working with the serial class and how it is going to pertain to some of the programming that happens with the Arduino API. This can help us to get so much done with some of the coding that we need, and can be an important class that will help us to get more done with our API.

Chapter 4 Connecting Switch

The push buttons or switches are going to connect two terminals that are open inside of a circuit.

Pull Down Resistor

The resistor is going to be used when you are working with electronic logic circuits so that it can make sure that the inputs that are on the Arduino panel are settled at the logic levels that are expected. In the event that there are external pieces of equipment that are not connected or are at a high impedance, then nothing is going to be attached to the input pin. This does not mean that it is a logical zero. The pull-down resistor is going to be connected to the ground and the proper pin on the device.

One example would be for the resistor in the circuit to be connected between the supply voltage and the microcontroller pin. In these circuits, the switch is going to be closed while the microcontroller input is high. However, when the switch is open, the resistor is going to pull the input voltage down so that it can prevent an undefined state of the input.

The resistor has to have a massive resistance over the impedance of the logic circuit, or it is going to pull the voltage down lower than it is supposed to be which is going to cause the input voltage to remain at a low value no matter where the switch is.

Components

1. LED (1)
2. Arduino Uno panel (1)

3. 4.7 k ohm resistor (1)

4. *330 ohm resistor (1)*

Code

// constants are not going to change they are going to be used to set the pin digital representations

Const int buttons pin = 8 // the digital representation of the push button pin

Const int led pin = 2 ; // the LED pin

// variable will change

Int button state = 0 ; // variable for reading the button status

Void setup () {

// initialize the LD pin as an output

Pin mode (led pin, output) ;

// initialize push button as an input ;

Pin mode (button pin, input0 ;

}

Void loop () {

// read the state of the push button value ;

Button state = digital read (button pin) ;

// check if the push button has been pushed

```
// if yes, then the button state will be high
If (button state == high) {
// turn LED on ;
Digital write (led pin , high) ;
} else {
// turn LED off
Digital write (led pin , low) ;
}
}
```

Chapter 5 Temperature Sensor

The temperature sensor is going to be a precision integrated circuit of temperature pieces of equipment that are going to contain an output voltage linearly proportional to the Centigrade temperature.

The LM35 device is going to have advantages over the linear temperature sensors that are calibrated to Kelvin so that the user is not required to deduct an extensive and continuous voltage from the output to get the Centigrade scaling. This device will not demand any additional calibration from outside sources or trim with a view to obtaining maximum accuracy. Most accuracies are going to be a fourth off either direction.

Technical Specifications

1. Suitable for applications that are remote
2. Will be calibrated for Celsius
3. Is going to be rated for temperatures between -55 and 150.
4. *Linear to a + 10 -mV/ degree Celsius scale*
5. Half a degree ensured accuracy.

Components

1. LM35 sensor (1)
2. Breadpanel (1)
3. Arduino Uno R3 (1)

Code

This is the code that you are going to place in the Arduino sketch program after you have created a more up to date file.

```
Float temp ;

Int temp pin = 1 ;

Void setup () {

Serial begin (8999) ;

Void loop () {

Temp = analog read (temp pin) ;

// read analog volt from sensor and save to variable temp

Temp = temp * 3.939403021 ;

// convert the analog volt to its tempt equivalent

Serial print (temperature = ) ;

Serial print (temp) ; // show temperature value

Serial print ( F ) ;

Serial print in () ;

Delay ( 300) ; // update sensor reading each one second

}
```

Notes on the code

1. Connect the GND to the GND that is located on the Arduino
2. Make sure that you connect the positive Vs. to the positive 5V that you can find on your panel.

3. Connect the V out to the analog 0 that is on the Arduino board.

The result that you are going to see is the temperature displayed on the serial port monitor which is updated each second.

Water Detector and Sensor

The water sensor brick is going to be designed for detecting water. This is going to be most often used to sense predetermined markers such as any leaks or even water levels.

When you are choosing to connect the water sensor to the Arduino panels, the sensor is going to be able to detect any measurement of water. It can accurately measure the level, presence, volume, or even if there is a complete lack of water. This is a great feature and even has the ability to remind the owner when it is time to water household plants!

You will be able to connect the water sensor to the eighth pin on the Arduino board.this pin is going to enlist an LED that enables us to identify when the sensor has come been exposed to water of any level.

Components

1. 330 ohm resistor (1)
2. Breadpanel (1)
3. Led (1)
4. *Arduino Uno R3 (1)*
5. Water sensor (1)

Procedure

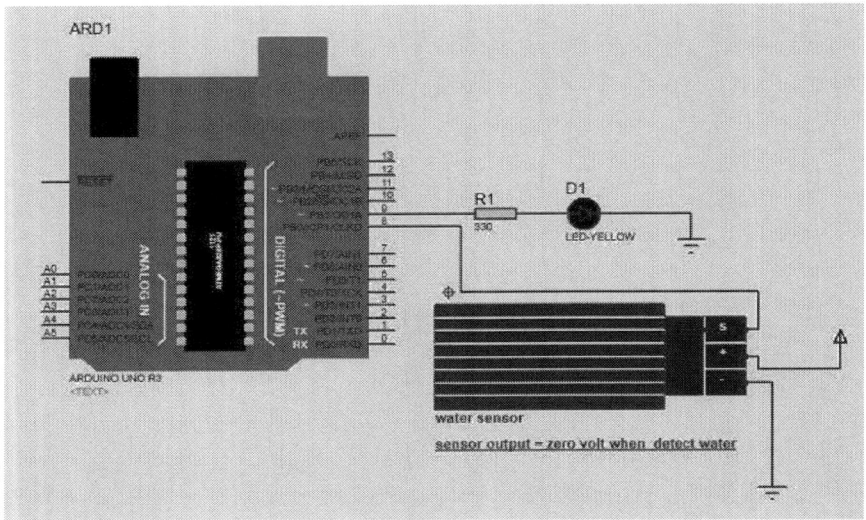

Code

define grove water sensor 9 // attach water sensor to Arduino digital pin 8

#define LED 9 // attach an LED to pin 9

Void setup () {

Pin mode (grove water sensor, input) ; // the water sensor will be an input

Pin mode (led, output) ; // the led will be an output

}

Notes on the code

There are going to be three terminals for the water sensor, and it is going to connect as follows.

1. The LED will be connected to the digital pin 9
2. The positive Vs. willl be tied to the positive side of the five volts.
3. The GND will be connected to the GND on the panel.
   4. *The S will be attached to the eight pin on the Arduino board.*

At the point in time that the sensor picks up any water, it is going to cause pin eigh to become weak, and the LED to be turned on.

PIR Sensor

A PIR sensor is going to allow you pick up motions, in other words, it is going to be a motion sensor. The sensor will detect movement inside of the sensors range. You are commonly going to find these sensors outside of homes and businesses. PIR is going to stand for passive infrared, pyroelectric, or IR motion sensor.

Here are some of the advantages of having a PIR sensor.

1. Does not wear out
2. Small
3. Easy to use
   4. *Has an extensive lens range*

5. Low power
6. Easy to interface
7. Low power

8. *Inexpensive*

A PIR is going to be made of pyroelectric sensors that are going to be located in a round metal can that contains a rectangular crystal in the center. This sensor is going to be able to detect varying levels of infrared radiation. Everything is going to emit some level of radiation. However, the hotter something is, the more radiation it is going to emit. The motion sensor is going to detect the change on the move and not just IR levels. The two halves of the panel are going to snap together which is going to cancel each other out. But, if one half gets more or less IR than the other, the output will end up being high or low.

A PIR is going to be adjustable in the settings while containing a header that is installed on the third pin.

For a lot of the basic projects that you can make to detect a human presence is going to use a PIR sensor. Keep in mind that a PIR is not going to tell you how many people are there or how close to the sensor they are. The lens is going to be fixed in such a way that it can sweep a distance.

Components

1. PIR sensor MQ3 (1)
2. Breadpanel (1)
3. Arduino Uno R3 (1)

Procedure

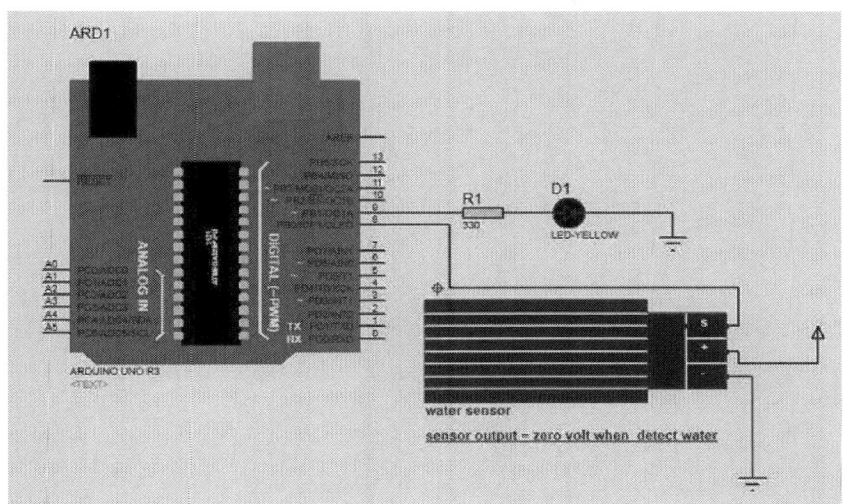

Code

#define pir pin 2

Int calibration time = 30 ;

Long unsigned int low in ;

Long unsigned int pause = 4000 ;

Boolean lock low = true ;

Boolean take low time ;

```
Int pir value = 0 ;

Void setup () {

Serial begin ( 9600) ;

Pin mode (pir pin, input) ;

}

Void look () {

Pir sensor () ;

}

Void pir sensor () {

if (digital read (pir pin ) == high ) {

if (lock low) {

pir value = 1;

lock low = false ;

serial print in (motion detected) ;

delay (60) ;

}

Take low time = true ;

}

If (digital read (pir pin) == low {
```

```
If (take low time ) {

Low in = millis() ; take low time = false ;

}

If (!locklow && millis () – lowin > pause) {

Pirvalue = 0 ;

Locklow = true ;

Serial print in (motion ended) ;

Delay (60)

}

}
```

Notes on code

There are three terminals for the pir.

1. The GND will be connected to the GND
2. The positive VCC will be connected to the positive side of the five volts
3. The out will be tied to the second pin on the panel.

You are going to be able to adjust the sensor sensitivity and delay time with two variable resistors that you can find at the bottom of the panel. After the sensor detects motion, the Arduino is going to send you a message to inform you that it has detected motion. The pir sensor is going to be delayed for some time to check if there is any more up to date motion. In the event that there is no more up to date motion detected, the panel will send you a message telling you so.

Chapter 6 Using the Stream Class

This is a topic that is going to be so important to what we are trying to do with some of our work that it really did deserve its own chapter to help us get the work done. While this one is still going to work with the API of Arduino that we talked about before it is going to be pretty broad and will talk about a lot of different parts, so we are going to break off here and work with the stream class, which also allows us to work with strings along the way.

The stream class is going to be a fairly simple concept even though it is really important to work with. The stream class on its own is going to be based on using reading information from a certain source, and then having this as how you make up your own sketch. Because the stream is all about reading the data, it is also important that we talk about working with a mouse and keyboard with the Arduino board in this chapter, even though we may think that these are not going to be related directly to the stream class that we are working with.

When you decide to work with the data, especially when you are readying the data, you will find that there are times when we need to work with sets of characters that are longer, like a sentence. The idea of strings is going to give you the chance to do this on our board. Strings are going to basically just be sets of character values that will be linked together like with an array. This means that they are going to be contiguous in the memory, and the computer is going to see them as one large and interconnected unit. Working with the strings means that we need to learn how to manipulate these units as well as our abilities will allow.

On its own, it is going to be pretty simple. Thought to work with. Strings are just going to be what we know as character arrays. That means that we are still working with some of the C-style strings, which are going to be strings that have abstraction at a very low level. For example, in a lot of the newer programming languages, the strings are not going to be revealed in their character as a character array. Instead of doing this, they are going to be treated as an abstract object instead. Even if they are considered a character array, they will be treated in this manner.

A string is going to be composed of the n + 1 characters, where n is going to be the number of letters that is in the string in general. So, for example, the size of a string for the word "hello" would end up being the six characters. The reason for this is because the string is going to end in a null terminating character, which is going to indicate to us that the end of the array has been reached and that it can be ended.

You are able to go through and define a string in the same manner that you would an array. You are able to also make them bigger than the string that you plan to have them contain. When you go through the process of defining an array you may give it a value right of the bat, but you can also just define the size and expand them out at a later time. this also makes strings, more dynamic and can allow us to change them up later on when we rewrite some of the data that is inside of that string.

This information is going to be useful to a programmer who is just getting started because these strings are going to be fundamental and important to any of the programs that you use that handle information, especially those that are going to handle the input and the output of the file. We have already spent some time looking at this, now, but we also need to go ahead and learn how we are able to define our string. The code that we are able to use for this one will be below:

char myString[6] = "hello";

You can then spend some time referring to this entire string at a later point with the name of the character. Most of the data that is worked with by the board is going to be worked with in terms of how many bytes it is, and most of the actual textual data is going to be worked with in terms of C strings because it is easy to parse these characters when you would like.

It is important that we go over all of these parts so that we learn and develop the right ideas that we need when it is time to treat the strings in this kind of programming and we see what we are able to do with some of these parts as well. Let's dive a bit more into this to see how it will work.

The Serial

While you are not necessarily able to implement the stream class in itself, you are able to go through and implement some of the derivatives of it, and this is where we are going to find a lot of the utility that we need. The serial class that we are going with here is going to be an extension of what we are able to do with the stream class, and it is going to help us to communicate with some of the other devices that we want, such as the computer.

The serial is going to be enacted through both the port on the Arduino for the Serial, as well as on the link for the USB on the computer. We are going to then look at some of the functions that are available with the Serial class, making it easier for you to use this kind of thing and get the most out of this resource along the way as well:

1. Serial.begin(rate): you are already familiar with how this one is going to work. It is a good one to use to help us start out the serial transmission of our data. You are also able to specify the specific rate of the data transmission that you are getting and see it in bits per second.

2. Serial.end): This function is going to allow us to end the communication through this. You can then go through and restart the communication by working with the Serial.begin() function that we did before. While the communication is disabled for whatever purpose, you are able to use the serial pins for generalized entry and exit of the data.

3. Serial.find(string): This is the one that is going to search for the given string within the data that is provided by the Serial. If the string is found, then the method is going to return true. If the string is not found, then the method is going to return the output of false to us.

4. Serial.findUntil(string, OPTIONAL endString): This one is going to take some time to look for a specific string within a

serial buffer, until either the string is found or the specified terminating string is found. If the target string is found, then the method is going to return true to us. If the terminating string is found or if the method times out, then you are going to get a return of false.

5. Serial.flush(): This one is going to all you time to halt a process until all of the data that is being sent to the serial has been sent.

6. Serial.parseFloat(): This function is going to work for us by returning the first floating point number to be provided with the serial stream. It is often going to be brought to an end with any character that is not seen as a floating point.

7. Serial.parseInt(): This one is going to be able to work by returning the first integer number to be provided by the serial stream. It is going to be brought to an end by the first character that you are working with that isn't a digit.

8. Serial.peek(): This one is going to return the very next character that should be imported by the serial buffer. However it is not going to remove any of the character from the bugger. This makes it a bit different than he Serial.read() method that we will talk about soon. This means that you are just going to be able to see which of the characters are coming next.

9. Serial.pint(value, OPTIONAL format): You are able to specify the format as well as an option. Otherwise, the integers are going to print as decimals by default. The floats

157

are going to print with two decimal places by default, and so on. You are able to send strings or characters as is to the print statement, and it is going to do the printing that you need without any issues.

10. Serial.pintln(value, OPTIONAL format): This one is going to allow you to prin out some of the values, just like we would expect with some of the other print methods out there.

11. Serial.read(): This one is going to be able to read the data that is showing up through your serial port. This is going to be added to some of the incoming stream of serial data and it is known as the serial buffer. When you read from this buffer, the information will then be destroyed, so we need to make sure that we are saving the data to a variable if we wish to reuse it at one point or another.

12. Serial.readBytes: This one is going to help us read in the characters from the serial port to the buffer. You are able to determine the number of bytes that you would like to see read. Your buffer has to be an array that is a byte or a char.

13. Serial.readBytesUntil: This one is going to work on reading the characters from the serial port, either until the given number of bytes has been read through on there, or until the chosen terminating character is read through as well. In either case, the method will then be able to terminate.

14. Serial.write(): This one is going to write out the data to the serial port. But this method is only going to send over data that is binary to the serial port. If you need to send over other kinds of data, like ASCII, you will need to work with the print method instead.

15. Serial.serialEvent(): The last method that we are going to take some time looking at is this one. Whenever the data you need comes to be available for use with your port of he serial, then this is going to be the function that is called. You can then use this function to help us read the data from the serial port.

As we can see here, we have spent a good deal of time talking about a lot of different topics, especially the functions that we are able to use when we are working with the serial class and how it is going to pertain to some of the programming that happens with the Arduino API. This can help us to get so much done with some of the coding that we need, and can be an important class that will help us to get more done with our API.

Chapter 7 Calculated Digital Representations

To generate calculated digital representations, you will use the calculated digital representation functions. You are going to have two functions to choose from.

1. Calculated ()

2. CALCULATED SEED (SEED)

Calculated Seed (Seed)

This function will reset the pseudocalculated digital representation generator. Even though the dispersion of the digital representations that are returned by the determined function, therefore, making them truly calculated while the sequence becomes predictable. You are going to have to reset the generator to the estimated value. In the event that you have an analog pin that is unconnected, it is going to pick up calculated commotion from the environment that is around the panel. This means that radio waves, electromagnetic interference, and cosmic rays can cause the generator to malfunction.

Example

Calculated seed (analog read (4)) ; //calculatedly pick from the commotion from analog pin 6

Calculated ()

The calculated function is going to create pseudo calculated digital representations.

Syntax

Long calculated (max) // it generates calculated digital representations from zero to max

Long calculated (min, max) // it generates calculated digital representations from min to max

Example

Long rand digital representation ;

Void setup () {

Serial. Begin (4329) ;

// if analog input pin zero is unconnected, calculated analog

// commotion will cause the call to calculated seed () to generate

// different seed digital representations every time that your sketch executes code

// calculated seed () will then shuffle the calculated function

Calculated seed (analog read (1)) ;

}

Void loop () {

// print a calculated digital representation from zero to two hundred and ninety-nine

Serial. Print ("calculated1 =") ;

Rand digital representation = calculated (301) ;

Serial. Println (rand digital representation) ; // print a calculated digital representation from zero to two hundred and ninety-nine.

Serial print ("calculated 2") ;

Rand digital representation = calculated (29, 39) ; // print a calculated digital representation from twenty-nine to thirty-nine

Serial. Print ln (rand digital representation) ;

Delay (29) ;

}

Bits

A bit is going to be a binary digit.

Any binary system that you use is going to use at least two digits, one and zero.

The bit system will work like the decimal digital representation system is going to work, because the digital representations will not hold the same value, the significance of a bit is going to depend on where you locate it in the digital representation line for binary digital representations. Take for example the decimal digital representation three hundred and three is going to be the same digital representations, but they are going to have different values.

Bytes

Bytes are going to consist of eight bits.

In the event that bits are represented by digits, then you can safely assume that a byte will be represented by a digital representation.

All mathematical equations can be completed with a byte.

The digits of a byte are not going to have the same significance.

The leftmost bit is going to have the greatest value, and it is going to be known as the most significant bit or MSB. On the opposite end, it is going to be referred to as the least important bit.

Being that there will be eight ones and zeros that are going to be one byte, at least two hundred and fifty-six of them are going to be used in various ways. The larger decimal digital representation is going to be shown by using a byte which will be two hundred and fifty-five.

163

Chapter 8 Understanding the Arduino Framework

In this chapter, we're going to actually start looking at the code which fuels Arduino. At this point, we are assuming that you have your Arduino unit and you've got it set up and linked to your computer. This is the first step.

The second step is to get an Arduino compatible IDE. For most beginners and novices, the ones supplied by Arduino themselves will be more than enough. You can navigate to their website and either download the desktop IDE or use the web-based IDE. Either one will work perfectly fine.

So, from here, we need to talk about the structure of sketches.

An Arduino sketch has two basic components that make it up: the 'setup' function and the 'loop' function. Both are essential to the overall functioning of the Arduino sketch, and so you need to make sure that every sketch you run has them. Your sketches, of course, are not limited to just these functions, and you can expand with more functions at ease as we described back in the C chapter.

The Arduino 'language,' so to speak, is just an extension of C and C++, which means that C and C++ coding conventions will work within them, as well as all of the things that we described previously. This makes programming your Arduino unit relatively easy.

The Arduino 'language' is actually a library with various different definitions and functions that are tailored to the Arduino.

This is how the most basic of Arduino programs look, in terms of structure:

void setup()

{

// code within

}

void loop()

{

// code within

}

The setup function should be just after the declaration of variables at the start of your sketch. It will always be the first function that your Arduino unit runs, so pay careful attention. You must have your setup function, even if there is nothing within it.

You use the setup function to do things like initializing Arduino relevant variables, like your pin modes. In other words, any necessary setup that you have to do to get everything up and running, those functions should be called from within your setup function.

Do note that not necessarily all of your variables must be declared here. Variables should generally be declared within their primary function or in the global scope. If you fail to define a function at these levels, you won't be able to use it where you want it to. For example, if you defined a variable within the setup function, you wouldn't be able to use it within your loop function since it was defined within another function and isn't global.

The loop function does pretty much exactly what it sounds like: it loops over and over until the program is brought to an end. When the program finally is brought to an end, the loop ends. Programs are generally brought to an end by cutting off power to your Arduino unit, so there isn't much of a way to exit the Arduino loop function. This is the primary function of your program, and everything happens from here.

Consider the fact that when you program something like an Arduino gadget, it really is just looping some function over and over every second, even if that loop is just something like waiting to receive input and then responding respectively when said input is given.

In terms of actual Arduino code from the framework, there are a few that you really need to know at this point.

Constants

Constants are a foundational part of Arduino programming because they allow you to make comparisons or assign certain things easily. Constants are variables which are predefined and do not change. They can be used as references in other functions used within the language.

Two constants are 'TRUE' and 'FALSE.' This harkens back to the language on *Booleans*. TRUE here is defined as anything other than zero, where FALSE is zero.

Two more are 'HIGH' and 'LOW.' These refer to the voltage being given to the pin, and the respective pin levels. HIGH refers to a pin which is 'ON' and which is receiving 5 volts while LOW refers to a pin which is 'OFF' and is receiving zero volts. This is used most often when you are either giving or receiving data from digital pins.

The other two constants that you need to know at this point are 'INPUT' and 'OUTPUT,' which merely allow you to define the mode of something and whether it is for incoming data or outgoing data.

Functions

There are some different functions that are inherent to Arduino programming that we need to cover. While a large amount of Arduino functions will vary depending upon the gadgets you have and the project that you're specifically trying to tackle, there are nonetheless manifold important

The first is *pinMode*, which takes the arguments of *pin* and *mode*. Pin is the respective integer of the given pin, where mode is either OUTPUT or INPUT, as we just said. Therefore, it ties in perfectly to what we were just discussing with the constants. This function will always be called within your setup function.

The next is *digitalRead()*, which takes an argument of a given *pin*, either as a constant or a variable. This will read in a value from a given pin and return either HIGH or LOW, this indicates either true/false, on/off, or 5v/0v.

The next is *digitalWrite*, which takes the arguments of a pin as well as HIGH or LOW, which will essentially turn a given pin on or off.

The next is *analogRead*, which accepts an argument of a given *pin* and will take a value from the analog in pins. It will return an integer value instead of HIGH or LOW.

After that is *analogWrite*, which will take the arguments of *pin* and *value*. *AnalogWrite* allows you to write what is essentially an analog value to a given pin. The value can be from 0 to 255, and the size of the number will indicate how often the signal sent is either 5 or 0 volts; a larger number indicates that the charge will more often be 5 volts than 0 volts. This works in a wave manner and will, therefore, act as a means to regulate how much power is being sent to the given pin.

After the read and write functions is the *delay* function, which pauses the program. It takes an argument of milliseconds, either as a variable or a constant. It will cause a pause in that length.

Beyond that is *millis()* which just returns the number of milliseconds that have passed since the current sketch started as a long. This number resets after several hours.

After that are the min and max functions, which take two arguments both and return either the smaller or larger number respectively. They accept numbers regardless of data type.

After that is *randomSeed* which accepts a given integer as an argument. This creates a seed for a random number generator.

Beyond this are the two random functions. Given one argument, the random function will return any number from zero to the max value. Given two arguments, it will return a number between the two numbers given. You must use *randomSeed* before you use a random function.

The last two functions we need to cover are the 'Serial' functions, which allow you to transmit serial data:

- *Serial.begin()* accepts an argument of the rate of transfer in bits per second. This is called in your setup function. The average rate is 9600 bits per second, so when in doubt, just use this.
- *Serial.println()* accepts an argument of any given data and will then print this to the Serial Monitor.

Chapter 9   Learn   the   Implementation   of Algorithms

In this chapter, we're going to discuss the implementation of algorithms in Arduino programming. Often, algorithms are understated in terms of their importance to Arduino programming, but using them, you're able to do many things that you wouldn't be able to otherwise.

An algorithm is, for lack of a better term, a way of standardizing a sort of procedure. We're going to be discussing two different types of algorithms and how they relate to Arduino programming, as well as discuss in both a theoretical and a practical sense how they can be implemented.

We first will look at the bubble sort algorithm and discuss sorting in relation to Arduino programming. Bubble sorting is the simplest form of sorting, but it will give you a decent look into algorithmic programming and a greater example of how algorithms actually are in practice.

The second thing that we will look at is a Bayesian probability algorithm which is important in statistical programming. Bayesian probability is also used to determine "true probability," which is probability that takes into account false positives and false negatives. We're going to be discussing why probability algorithms may be useful in Arduino programming and how you may find yourself using them in the future depending upon your various different projects.

Let's start by looking at sorting and thinking about when it could be useful to us as Arduino programmers. Sorting is the idea of taking some set of data and then filtering through it and moving things around accordingly. Let's say, for example, that we had an array of ten values. There are times where we may need to sort these. While there do exist certain functions in the Arduino library for getting the minimum or maximum of two values, there is no built-in sorting function for an array, and there's no built-in way to obtain the largest and smallest values within an array.

This is an introduction to algorithmic thinking more than anything else because Arduino is a perfect proxy to building bigger and better technological systems based off of concepts such as artificial intelligence and the internet of things. More than that, algorithms come up in complex programs and having some idea as to how to break down what an algorithm needs to do and then implementing it is a first important step to developing some sort of methodology for programming algorithmically.

The sample language for this example will be C/C++, but the key concepts will remain the same across any language. This is the first time in this book that we're not going to be using pseudocode.

Let's first define an array of 10 random values. You can make them whatever. Here are mine:

int numbers[10] = { 39, 63, 10, 70, 23, 34, 63, 13, 76, 34 };

This is the first important step. Afterward, we need to define the how our algorithm will work. Let's think about this for a second.

What a bubble sort essentially does is look at any given value in an array and compare it to a number either immediately before or after it. If the number before or after is larger or smaller (implementation can vary), then the two numbers will be swapped.

This might seem straightforward: you simply iterate through the array and perform checks to see if a given element is larger than another, right?

Not quite. If you used a single loop to iterate through the array, you're not actually going to be accomplishing much of anything. Instead, you need to use two for loops. The first loop will denote what we can call our *active position*. This will move through every element in the array one by one and perform the necessary checks and swaps until an *n*th element has been checked.

After that, you'll use a second for loop. This creates an *active integer* and compares it against every other element in the array. This is the loop of action. The other is the loop of iteration.

Within the loop of action, we must, therefore, create some kind of check mechanism. We can do this by comparing the active integer against another element in the array. If the other element is smaller, the two elements will swap positions. This means that the smaller element will be pushed towards the front of the array.

By now, we can assume that this means we need two functions: a *sort* function which will contain the logic of our sort mechanism, and a *swap* function which can perform the swap of the two integers given their addresses in memory.

We can implement these two like so:

For the *swap* function, we're going to want it to take the argument of two pointer addresses. Within the function, it will then define a temporary placeholder variable which we can call *i*. The placeholder will be used to store the value of integer 1. Integer 1 will then assume the value of integer 2. Integer 2 then assumes the value of the placeholder, which is the old value of integer 1, meaning integer 1 and 2 have now effectively swapped positions. Here is how I would define this function:

void swap(int *p1, int *p2)
{
int i = *p1;
*p1 = *p2;
*p2 = i;
}

Easy peasy. The logic behind it is a little rough, but that's all an important part of the learning process!

Now, moving on beyond this, we're going to now work with our *sort* function. The sort function will create two iterative arrays. It will accept the arguments of the array's size and the array itself. It will iterate through these accordingly. Since we're comparing in a forward manner, the active position should only extend to the size of the array minus one element; otherwise, when the last element in the array is reached, there will be an element overflow error, and the program will crash (if it executes at all.)

For the second for loop, we need to iterate according to the size minus the active position minus 1.

Within the second for loop, we need to define an if statement which checks to see whether the active integer is larger than the number immediately ahead of it. If it is, then the two swap positions, meaning we throw the memory addresses of the two to the swap function.

Here is how I would define this function:

void sort(int myArray[], int size)

{

for (int i = 0; i < size - 1; i++)
for (int j = 0; j < size - i - 1; j++)
if (myArray[j] > myArray[j+1])
swap(&myArray[j], &myArray[j+1]);

}

Again, it's not a terribly difficult algorithm, but it does require a bit of thought and is a decent introduction to algorithmic thinking if you've never done so before. To test this all, we can create a program with our test array that will do all of this, then print it out for us so that we can see if all is in working order:

#include <stdio.h>
*void swap(int *p1, int *p2)*
{
*int i = *p1;*

```c
*p1 = *p2;
*p2 = i;
}

void sort(int myArray[], int size)
{
for (int i = 0; i < size - 1; i++)
for (int j = 0; j < size - i - 1; j++)
if (myArray[j] > myArray[j+1])
swap(&myArray[j], &myArray[j+1]);
}

int main()
{
int numbers[10] = { 39, 63, 10, 70, 23, 34, 63, 13, 76, 34 };
int size = sizeof(numbers)/sizeof(numbers[0]);
sort(numbers, size);
for (int i = 0; i < size; i++)
{
printf("%d", numbers[i]);
}
}
```

Your end program should look somewhat like the one above. If so, then you've succeeded.

The next thing that we're going to discuss in an algorithmic sense is probability using a very rudimentary version of Bayes' theorem.

So what exactly is Bayes' theorem, and why is it useful as an Arduino programmer? Well, Bayes' theorem in and of itself is a way of determining true probability of a given situation based upon the likelihood that something has happened in the past. It takes into account various given rates and then returns a certain dimension based on those rates.

For this, we can take two events: event X and event Y. We then have P(X) which is the likelihood of X, and P(Y) which is the likelihood of Y. P(X|Y) is the likelihood of event X given that Y is true, and P(Y|X) is the likelihood of event Y if event X is true.

Let's say we're trying to find the likelihood of event X given that Y is true, and we have data related to event Y is X is true. Bayes' theorem then allows us to look at it like so:

P(X|Y) = P(Y|X)*P(X) / P(Y)

In other words, the probability of event X given that Y is true is equivalent to the probability of Y given that X is true multiplied by the probability of X, then all of this divided over the probability of Y.

Bayes' theorem is a little difficult to grasp if you aren't looking at it in an intuitive manner. Take, for example, spam filtering, which is a rather common application of Bayes' theorem in the world of computer science.

Let's say that event X is the likelihood that the message is spam, and event Y is the likelihood that it contains certain words flagged as spam. $P(X|Y)$ is the probability that it is spam given that it contains words flagged as spam. $P(Y|X)$ is the probability that a certain word flagged as spam will be in a spam message. $P(X)$ is the probability that any given message is spam, and $P(Y)$ is the probability that the words within are flagged for spam.

Therefore, we can render the equation something like this:

The probability that a message is spam based on flagged words *is equivalent to* the probability that the flagged words are in a spam message *multiplied by* the probability that a message is spam, *all divided by* the probability that flagged words are spam.

This yields:

P(spam|words) = P(words|spam)*P(spam) / P(words)

This could be rendered algorithmically rather simply, and it's a very rudimentary probability equation. However, this does give us a solid starting point. The equation, too, can be mostly given over without much thought given to the conversion process.

For this, we're going to need just one function which returns *x given y* based upon *y given x*, *y*, and *x*. We'll call this function *calc_prob*. We will use this function to return a double value which will be saved to a variable and printed out to the console.

The finished code would look something like this:

```
#include <stdio.h>
double calc_prob(double ygivenx, double x, double y)
{
return (ygivenx * x) / y;
}

int main()
{
double spam = 3100, words = 6888, wordsgivenspam = 7000;
double spamgivenwords = calc_prob(wordsgivenspam, spam, words);
printf("%.2f", spamgivenwords);
}
```

With that, you've written your second algorithm. Probability algorithms become massively useful when you need your Arduino programs to be able to act predictively. For example, you could use your Arduino to model certain situations or react accordingly. While it's not powerful enough for hardcore number crunching, it will definitely be powerful enough for basic probability equations. This, for example, is nothing too intensive. So long as it can retrieve information to form a dataset, you can use much of the information in this book to make highly reactive Arduino sketches that could, ideally, change the world.

The purpose of introducing these two algorithms was to give you insight as to how algorithms might impact your programming and how thinking algorithmically can be a major boon to your ability to program in the first place. Consider that the ability to mentally process and break apart certain functions is foundational to being able to think like a programmer, which - in the end - is what this book is trying to help you do.

Chapter 10 Troubleshooting

As you work on your projects, there are specific situations when there will be troubleshooting and debugging.

The more you use Arduino and electronics, the better you become and gain experience. This will end up making the whole process less painful. Don't be frustrated with the problems that you experience. It is much easy than the way it might look at the start.

Since each Arduino project consists of a hardware and software, there are many places to check when things go wrong. Therefore, when debugging, you need to consider these three aspects:

Understanding

You should strive to understand as much as you can in the way the parts you have in your project operate and how they should contribute to the final project. This method will allow you to develop ways in which you can check every component independently.

Simplify and segment

In the ancient Romans, they had what we call divide and rule type of government. You need to break down your project into different components using your intelligence to determine which part of a given function starts and ends.

Exclusion and Certainty

While investigating, you need to check each component individually to ensure that you are sure every component works by itself. You will slowly develop your confidence and note the parts of the project that are doing well and areas that you should fix.

Debugging is the term we refer to the process of fixing errors in software. It was first used by Grace Hopper back in the 1940s. This was the time when computers were majorly electrochemical. It is believed one computer stopped working after an actual insect found its way inside.

However, many of today's bugs are not physical like in this case. Instead, they are virtual and invisible. This means they call for more time and that process can be boring.

Testing the Board

What if the first example of blinking an LED failed to work? That would possibly be frustrating. Let us see what you can do.

Before you throw complains at your project, you need to ascertain that several things are in the right place. This is similar to the way airline pilots follow when they run through a list of things to make sure that there will be no problems when the plane takes off.

The first thing you need to do is to plug your USB into your computer:

- *Verify that the PC is on. This might look obvious, but you could forget to turn on your computer. When the green light labeled PWR lights up, this implies that the computer is powering the board. However, if the LED looks faint, then something is wrong with the power. You can*

> *change the USB cable and check the computer USB port as well as the Arduino USB plug port on your computer.*

- *If you are using a new Arduino, the yellow LED labeled L will start to blink.*

- Now, if you had been using an external source of power and you have connected an old Arduino. Just ensure that the power supply is inserted in and the jumper labeled as SV1 has been connected to the two pins that are close to the external power supply connector.

Another point you need to note is when you are experiencing problems with some sketches, and you want to verify that the board is working. Open and transfer the blink an LED example in the IDE to the board. The onboard LED has to blink in a regular pattern. If you follow all the above steps, then you should be confident that the Arduino is going to work correctly.

Test the Breadboard Circuit

To test your breadboard circuit, join the board to your breadboard by executing a jumper from the GND and 5V connections right between the negative and positive rails of the breadboard. When the green PWR LED goes off, remove the wires. This shows that there exists an error in the circuit and there is a short circuit. A short-circuit leads to an excessive current which cuts off the current as a mechanism to protect your computer.

However, if you are concerned that you might destroy your computer, remember that most machines have safety mechanisms. Besides, the Arduino board has an independently powered USB hub.

If you have a short circuit, it is essential to apply the divide and conquer approach. What you require to do is to look for each sensor in the project and connect each sensor one at a time.

The first thing that you need to begin with is the power source. Review each part of the circuit to ensure that power flows through it. Work procedurally and perform a single change in every step.

Any time you are in the process of debugging and things do not seem to go well, the best thing to do is to handle everything systematically. This is very important because it will help you fix the problem, and that is why it is crucial that you update one at a time.

In addition, do not forget that each debugging process will stick in your head. You will develop an understanding of some of the things to fix up when you encounter a problem. In addition, after some time you will become an expert at doing it.

IDE problems

There are times when you might experience problems with the Arduino IDE, primarily if you are working on Windows. If you receive an error when you double-click the Arduino Icon or nothing happens, you should attempt to execute the run.bat file, which is another option to start Arduino.

Windows users might again run into a problem if the operating system allocates the COM port to a COM10 or higher number to the Arduino.

If this takes place, you can let Windows assign a lower port number to the Arduino.

Look for Help Online

If you find yourself stuck entirely such that you are spending a lot of time trying to debug, it might be time to turn to the community of users at the Arduino forum. One of the best things, when you look for help online, is that you will always find someone ready to assist you if you can describe your problem correctly.

Develop a practice of cutting and pasting things into a search engine and wait to check the results if there is a person who has tried to solve it. Look around to discover a solution, nearly every problem you encounter must have an answer.

You, start with checking the main Arduino website before you can move to the playground. Another critical thing to note is before you begin your project, you should search in the playground for a few lines of code or circuit diagram to help you build your project.

Chapter 11 *Projects*

The Keyboard Instrument

With the help of some buttons, resistors and other devices, you will build a small musical keyboard.

Although you can join a few switches into a digital input and produce different types of tones, in this particular project, you will learn how to build a resistor ladder.

This is a method where you can read some switches by using an analog input. It is an essential technique if you have limited digital data. You will connect some parallel switches into the analog. When you touch each button, there will be a separate voltage level that will flow through the input pin. If you press down two buttons simultaneously, you will find a unique input that depends on the link between the two resistors arranged in parallel. The figure below shows a ladder and five switches.

Let's look at the circuit

1. *First, you have to connect the breadboard to the power and ground like the one we did in the previous examples. Hold one side of the piezo and join it to the ground. Connect the remaining side of the pin to your Arduino.*
2. *Arrange the switches on the breadboard the same way it has been done in the figure above. The pattern of the resistors and switches going into the analog input is the resistor ladder.*

Look for something to enclose your keyboard. Take a small cardboard piece that you can cut to fit your buttons. Mark the keys to help you remember the notes that have been triggered by every key.

3. *Take a small piece of paper that has holes that belong to the four buttons and the piezo. Decorate it so that it can resemble a piano keyboard.*

4. Place the paper on top of the buttons and piezo, and enjoy the creation.

The CODE

This program requires one to have different frequency values which you want to play when you touch the buttons. You can start with the frequencies for the

Parts labeled C, D, E, and F. To achieve this, you must create a variable called array.

An array holds different values of similar type; this can be the frequencies of a musical scale. They are a great tool to help one access information fast. If you want to declare an array, do the same way you declare a variable, but make sure the name follows with a pair of square brackets. The elements of the array remain in the curly brackets.

Anyone who would like to change the elements of the array has to first reference the individual elements by listing the name and index of the element. The index is the order by which things will appear in the array. The first index in an array is 0 and the next is 1. This order follows that trend until the last element is reached.

Creating an array of frequencies

Declare an array to store four notes. Make the array global by making the declaration before the start of the setup() function.

In the loop(), create a local variable to hold the reading of pin A0. Given that each switch has a different resistor value that connects to the source of power, there will be unique values. To see the values, use the line below

Serial.println(keyVal)

We have used an if...else statement to help us allocate every value to its particular tone. This program has used random figures for the size of the resistor. Do not use the exact figures in your program because resistors have some errors, this may fail to work in your case.

```
int buttons[6];
// set up an array with 6 integers

int buttons[0] = 2;
// give the first element of the array the value 2
```

```
1  int notes[] = {262,294,330,349};
```

```
2  void setup() {
3    Serial.begin(9600);
4  }
```

```
5  void loop() {
6    int keyVal = analogRead(A0);
7    Serial.println(keyVal);
```

```
8    if(keyVal == 1023){
9      tone(8, notes[0]);
10   }
```

Play notes that are similar to the analog value

Call the tone() after every if() statement call. The program tells the array to calculate the frequency to play if the value of AO is similar to the one in the if statements, you can allow the Arduino to play the tone. There is also a possibility that your circuit is noisy and the values can rise when you press the switch. Therefore, it is a good thing to use small values to validate.

If you apply the "&&," look for multiple statements to determine if it is correct. When you press the first button, the notes in the first element will play, touching the second button, the notes in the second element plays and the cycle continues.

To stop the note from playing you use the function noTone(). Just specify as a parameter the pin number you want to stop.

However, in case you have resistors close to one another like in the example program, you should hear sounds originating from the piezo when you press the buttons. If you don't understand, navigate to the serial monitor and make sure that every button is within the range of the notes in the conditional if statement. If you hear a stuttering sound, increase the scale a bit.

Press several buttons simultaneously, and see the type of values that appear in the serial monitor. Use the new values to generate more sounds. Test as many frequencies and expand the musical output.

The tone() function is the best when you want to generate sounds. However, it has some limitations. For instance, the function can only create square waves but not smooth sine waves. Square waves are different from typical waves. While you are about to begin your band, remember that only a single tone can play every time and the function tone interfaces with the analogWrite() on pins 11 and 3.

Note

Finally, remember that arrays are important when you have a similar type of information that you want to classify together. You access arrays using index numbers that point to distinct elements. Resistor ladders provide the right circuit to channel digital signals into a system by inserting into an analog input.

DIGITAL HOURGLASS

In this project, you are going to learn how to build a digital hourglass that switches on an LED after 10 minutes. This will help you know the time you spend working on your projects.

So far you have seen that when you want to make something happen at a specific time interval, you have to apply the delay() function. This is convenient but at the same time limited in what it can achieve. When the delay() is called, it stops the flow of current based on the time of delay. This means that there is no input and output during the delay. Besides, delays are not the best to use to monitor time. If your goal were to do something after every 20 seconds, a delay of 20 seconds would be very long.

The millis() function comes in to provide a much better solution to this problem. The function will record the time the Arduino has been on.

Up to now, we have declared variables as an int. An int consists of a 16-bit number that contains values in the range "-32,768 and 32,767." That is a large number, but not when the Arduino is making a count of 1000 times a second using the millis() function, in just a few minutes you will be out of space. The long data type can store a 32-bit number.

Given that time cannot run back to produce negative numbers, we declare an unsigned long variable to store millis() time. A data type of unsigned type can only be positive. In addition, an unsigned long can extend to 4,294,967,295. This is sufficient space to store time for even 50 days. So, if you compare the function millis() to a given value, you can tell if a certain amount of time has ended.

So when you rotate your hourglass, a tilt switch will update its state, and that begins a different LED cycle.

The tilt switch operates the same way as a normal switch where it has an on and off sensor. In this project, you will use it as a digital signal. Something unique about tilt switches is the way they determine the orientation. Usually, it contains a small cavity with a metal ball. If adjusted correctly, the ball will roll to one particular side of the cavity and join two leads in the breadboard.

1. *The first thing is to connect the power and ground to your breadboard*
2. *The next thing to do is to join the six LEDs to the digital pins 2-7 through the anode. The LEDs have to be connected to the ground through a resistor.*
3. *Connect one lead of the tilt switch to the 5V. The remaining part should be connected to the ground.*

Create a stand using the cardboard and allow power to flow to the Arduino using a battery. You can build a cover that has some numeric displays close to the lights.

Tilt switches are cheap and affordable components to help one tell the orientation of something. Another example of tilt sensors are the accelerometers. In addition, they are quite expensive. If you are only interested to see whether something is up or down, you should go with the tilt sensors.

The Code

Define a constant

In this project, you will need to have several global variables so that you can have everything work. To begin with, define a constant called switchPin.

Declare a variable to store time

Declare an unsigned long variable. This variable will record the last time the LED changed.

Declare variables to hold inputs and outputs

Define variables for both the switch state and previous switch state. The input and output variables will help make a comparison of the switch's position from one state to the next. Declare a variable called *led*. This will make the next LED to switch on. You can start with pin 2.

Variable declaration showing the interval between two events

The last variable to define is the interval between each LED. This is the long datatype.

Determine the time the program started.

Once the loop() begins, you can find the time the Arduino has been on using the function millis() and place it in a variable called currentTime.

Determine the time that has elapsed since the first loop()

With the help of an if() statement, you need to determine whether time has reached to switch on the LED. Perform some mathematical operations by subtracting the currentTime from the original time and test to see if it is more than the interval variable.

Switch on the LED, and prepare for the next

The previousTime displays the last time the LED was on. The moment the previousTime is set, switch on the LED and increase the led variable. If you pass the time interval again, the next LED lights up.

Find out whether all the lights are on

Create another if statement in the program to help you determine whether the LED on pin marked 7 is on. Make sure you do not attempt anything with it.

Towards the end of the loop, save the state of the switch in the prevSwitchState, and compare it with the value you receive for the switchState in next loop().

If you are done with programming the board, look at the time in the clock. Once 10 minutes pass, the first LED has to be turned on. After every 10 minutes, a new light will display. After an hour, all the six light will turn on.

Chapter 12 Spend Time Thinking Outside the Box (and the Arduino)

In this chapter, we're going to talk about how creative thinking and spending time away from Arduino programming both might enable you to be a better Arduino programmer in the end.

This may not make a lot of sense, but the fact is that both of these ideas have a lot of credence. No masterful painter ever got to their mastery by working simply with oils, though they may strongly *prefer* to work with oils. The same applies here: without thinking outside the box and working outside of your comfort zone, you're going to be missing out on a lot of different things that would lead you to become a better programmer and a better Arduino builder in general.

Here's a simple fact for you: all of creativity is based on the way that the brain processes inputs and outputs. Although there is some variety of spontaneous components, you can only ever invent things which are based on those things you've already learned or those things you've already been made aware of. Your ideas will almost always be based on those inputs that you've already dealt with in the past instead of being based on things that are spontaneously generated in terms of new ideas.

Spontaneous generation of ideas can lead to really cool and abstract things, but even the most spontaneous ideas are based on learned stimuli, from a psychological perspective. In other words, no thought that you've ever had has been completely original, because all of your thoughts are formed by the world around you and the unique way in which you happen to process all of that information.

If you want to be a good Arduino programmer, you really need to not stop at Arduino programming. For example, the fundamental languages which power the Arduino language itself, C and C++, have been used for a massive variety of different utilities in the nearly forty years that they've been around. At some point in these languages' long histories, there has been something done that you've never even thought of, surely.

It is by taking in these inputs and getting this practice that you enable yourself to become a better programmer and do more.

I think that a good example would harken back to the phenomenon known as a Magic Mirror. Magic Mirrors are computer monitors which display information fed in by a Raspberry Pi, a microcomputer not too different from an Arduino through a tad bit more powerful and intended for different purposes. The monitor is tucked behind a one-sided mirror such that the information on the monitor displays on the reflective side of the mirror. What results is a mirror that is incredibly science fiction becoming a science reality.

The thing is that while the project itself is simple, the logic behind the program really isn't; for example, to display the data, a modified version of the Chromium browser is used. Within that Chromium browser, a custom page is built using HTML, CSS, and JavaScript (to retrieve information from the web).

It is through the knowledge of how to make these different things happen that a project as ambitious as the Magic Mirror was made possible. If one didn't have the knowledge of how to modify and recompile the Chromium browser, nor if they didn't have the knowledge on how to build web pages using HTML, CSS, and JavaScript, the project simply would have never happened; it would have remained science fiction.

In other words, you may have incredible ideas, but actually being able to take action to make them happen is an entirely different beast altogether. One thing is for certain: building up the knowledge required to, for example, build web pages or modify and recompile a web browser then write a bash script to automatically launch it upon the operating system starting up are things which go well beyond the scope of hobbyist programming for the Arduino.

You can ask for the help of other people, but that will only get you so far and nudge you along a little at a time. So what's the other option, then?

All of this chapter has been building up to this: your ability to program Arduino sketches and to make your dream projects happen is based on you, not programming in Arduino at all.

Programming is a common set of skills that usually transfer across projects, but as an Arduino programmer, you generally are not building these skills in the optimal way. Reading books like this one is a start because they teach you the underlying concepts to all of the computer science mumbo-jumbo that you're being fed, which hopefully acts to help make things click a little bit. But there are a lot of bigger concepts that you aren't going to pick up just within your Arduino IDE. These are things like working with APIs, learning how to read documentation, learning how to create header files or libraries to make your programs more modular, learning in general how to be a better programmer.

These are skills which you gain through continually challenging yourself and trying to come up with new things.

And this has a little perk tacked onto the end of it, too: if you try to work on new things, you will be inspired more often. You'll learn how to do things and start having ideas that you wouldn't have had otherwise, because you'll be enjoying new experiences and getting all sorts of new inputs. When you think about things you've never thought about before, your brain interprets this as a good thing - as a learning experience. This will expand your mind and make you more creative, in turn making you simultaneously a better programmer and a better tinkerer.

So in other words, if you want to be a good Arduino programmer, one of the best things that you can possibly do for yourself is to start working on projects that aren't Arduino-based. You need to be exposing yourself to new things and challenging yourself to become better all of the time.

Chapter 13 Troubleshooting

As you work on your projects, there are specific situations when there will be troubleshooting and debugging.

The more you use Arduino and electronics, the better you become and gain experience. This will end up making the whole process less painful. Don't be frustrated with the problems that you experience. It is much easy than the way it might look at the start.

Since each Arduino project consists of a hardware and software, there are many places to check when things go wrong. Therefore, when debugging, you need to consider these three aspects:

Understanding

You should strive to understand as much as you can in the way the parts you have in your project operate and how they should contribute to the final project. This method will allow you to develop ways in which you can check every component independently.

Simplify and segment

In the ancient Romans, they had what we call divide and rule type of government. You need to break down your project into different components using your intelligence to determine which part of a given function starts and ends.

Testing the Board

What if the first example of blinking an LED failed to work? That would possibly be frustrating. Let us see what you can do.

Before you throw complains at your project, you need to ascertain that several things are in the right place. This is similar to the way airline pilots follow when they run through a list of things to make sure that there will be no problems when the plane takes off.

The first thing you need to do is to plug your USB into your computer:

- Verify that the PC is on. This might look obvious, but you could forget to turn on your computer. When the green light labeled PWR lights up, this implies that the computer is powering the board. However, if the LED looks faint, then something is wrong with the power. You can change the USB cable and check the computer USB port as well as the Arduino USB plug port on your computer.
- If you are using a new Arduino, the yellow LED labeled L will start to blink.
- Now, if you had been using an external source of power and you have connected an old Arduino. Just ensure that the power supply is inserted in and the jumper labeled as SV1 has been connected to the two pins that are close to the external power supply connector.

Another point you need to note is when you are experiencing problems with some sketches, and you want to verify that the board is working. Open and transfer the blink an LED example in the IDE to the board.

The onboard LED has to blink in a regular pattern. If you follow all the above steps, then you should be confident that the Arduino is going to work correctly.

Test the Breadboard Circuit

To test your breadboard circuit, join the board to your breadboard by executing a jumper from the GND and 5V connections right between the negative and positive rails of the breadboard. When the green PWR LED goes off, remove the wires. This shows that there exists an error in the circuit and there is a short circuit. A short-circuit leads to an excessive current which cuts off the current as a mechanism to protect your computer.

However, if you are concerned that you might destroy your computer, remember that most machines have safety mechanisms. Besides, the Arduino board has an independently powered USB hub.

If you have a short circuit, it is essential to apply the divide and conquer approach. What you require to do is to look for each sensor in the project and connect each sensor one at a time.

The first thing that you need to begin with is the power source. Review each part of the circuit to ensure that power flows through it. Work procedurally and perform a single change in every step.

Any time you are in the process of debugging and things do not seem to go well, the best thing to do is to handle everything systematically. This is very important because it will help you fix the problem, and that is why it is crucial that you update one at a time.

In addition, do not forget that each debugging process will stick in your head. You will develop an understanding of some of the things to fix up when you encounter a problem. In addition, after some time you will become an expert at doing it.

IDE problems

There are times when you might experience problems with the Arduino IDE, primarily if you are working on Windows. If you receive an error when you double-click the Arduino Icon or nothing happens, you should attempt to execute the run.bat file, which is another option to start Arduino.

Windows users might again run into a problem if the operating system allocates the COM port to a COM10 or higher number to the Arduino. If this takes place, you can let Windows assign a lower port number to the Arduino.

Look for Help Online

If you find yourself stuck entirely such that you are spending a lot of time trying to debug, it might be time to turn to the community of users at the Arduino forum. One of the best things, when you look for help online, is that you will always find someone ready to assist you if you can describe your problem correctly.

Develop a practice of cutting and pasting things into a search engine and wait to check the results if there is a person who has tried to solve it. Look around to discover a solution, nearly every problem you encounter must have an answer.

You, start with checking the main Arduino website before you can move to the playground. Another critical thing to note is before you begin your project, you should search in the playground for a few lines of code or circuit diagram to help you build your project.

Conclusion

Thank you for making it through to the end!

The next step is to purchase the kind of Arduino board that you would like to work with and then go on from there. In the beginning of this guidebook we spent some time looking at what the Arduino board is all about and some of the different options that you are able to use in order to make it do the work that you would like. And picking out the board that is going to help you with some of the projects that you want to complete is going to be an important first step to focus on.

From there, it is time to go through the various steps that we spent our time on in this guidebook so that you can learn a bit about this language and what it is able to do for you. There are many beginners who are worried about learning any kind of coding at all, much less the Arduino language. But you will quickly find that this is a simple language that you are able to work with, one that will help you to see the best results in no time, and is designed for the student, or someone with no engineering or technical experience, to gain some experience on coding in the first place.

There are a lot of different parts that are going to come with this language, and being able to explore it some more, and learn from what is there, is going to make a big difference in the response that we are able to get, and how good we feel about some of our own coding prowess along the way. Don't be worried our scared about the topics that we are going to explore in this guidebook. You will find that they are easy and before long, you will be able to hook up the Arduino machine and get it to work on any project that you want.

In addition to some of those great benefits and the basics of the Arduino, we took it a bit further and looked at some of the things that you are able to do with this system when it comes to coding. We looked at many different parts such as how to turn it into a machine, how to work with the stream class and the Arduino API, and even how to create some of your own user defined functions along the way. all of this came together to help you learn some of the basics of your first coding language, and make it easier for you to get into this world in no time.

There are so many things that you are able to love when it comes to using the Arduino technology to help you out with some of the coding that you would like to accomplish. And getting started on it is easier than you may think. When you are ready to learn how to code, but you want a nice and simple method to use in order to do this, make sure to check out this guidebook to help you get started.

Printed by Amazon Italia Logistica S.r.l.
Torrazza Piemonte (TO), Italy